PENGUIN BOOKS

PRIMORDIAL SOUP

Grant Naylor is a gestalt entity occupying two bodies, one of which lives in north London, the other in south London. The product of a horribly botched genetic-engineering experiment, which took place in Manchester in the late fifties, they try to eke out two existences with only one mind. They attended the same school and the same university, but, for tax reasons, have completely different wives.

The first body is called Rob Grant, the second Doug Naylor. Among other things, they spent three years in the mid-eighties as head writers of *Spitting Image*; wrote Radio Four's award-winning series *Son of Cliché*; penned the lyrics to a number one single; and created and wrote *Red Dwarf* for BBC Television.

They have made a living variously by being ice-cream salesmen and shoe-shop assistants and by attempting to sell dodgy life-assurance policies to close friends. They also spent almost two years on the night shift loading paper into computer printers at a mail-order factory in Ardwick. They can still taste the cheese 'n' onion toasties.

Their favourite colour is orange. *Red Dwarf* was an enormous bestseller when published as a Penguin paperback in 1989. *Better Than Life* was the not-very-long-awaited sequel. Both are also published by Penguin in one volume entitled *Red Dwarf Omnibus*.

GRANT NAYLOR

———————

PRIMORDIAL SOUP

RED DWARF SCRIPTS

PENGUIN BOOKS

PENGUIN BOOKS

Published by the Penguin Group
Penguin Books Ltd, 27 Wrights Lane, London w8 5tz, England
Penguin Books USA Inc., 375 Hudson Street, New York, New York 10014, USA
Penguin Books Australia Ltd, Ringwood, Victoria, Australia
Penguin Books Canada Ltd, 10 Alcorn Avenue, Toronto, Ontario, Canada m4v 3b2
Penguin Books (NZ) Ltd, 182–190 Wairau Road, Auckland 10, New Zealand

Penguin Books Ltd, Registered Offices: Harmondsworth, Middlesex, England

First published in book form in Penguin Books 1993
5 7 9 10 8 6

Typeset by Datix International Limited, Bungay, Suffolk
Printed in England by Clays Ltd, St Ives plc

CONTENTS

Introduction   vii

Boring Technical Bit   ix

Polymorph   1

Marooned   24

Dimension Jump   45

Justice   75

Back to Reality   93

Psirens   121

List of Episode Credits   152

INTRODUCTION

Fundamentally, a Red Dwarf script is a battle plan for making a TV show, and as Napoleon Bonaparte once remarked, 'No battle plan ever survived contact with the enemy.' Actually, he didn't say that at all, but he did say something remarkably similiar in French, and his point was not lost. In Red Dwarf's case the enemy is what is possible, given a tight budget, a short production period and the physical laws of the natural universe.

The enemy is a prop that doesn't work. A guest star who can't say the word 'soup'. Another who can't say 'phenomenon'. Writing the stage direction 'Beach in Paradise', and finding yourself on a wet winter day in Rhyll, watching the rapidly bluing cast gratefully guzzling hot toddies in between takes, so their teeth don't hammer together like copulating woodpeckers, as the director wanders among the frozen crew, confidently announcing he can make it look sunny in the edit. The enemy is two radio-controlled skutters who pick up mini-cab transmissions half way through a scene in front of the studio audience and spontaneously attack Rimmer with a flurry of vicious pecks to his lower torso. The enemy is reality, and reality is, unfortunately, everywhere.

Contained herein are the battle plans for six episodes of Red Dwarf. From the third season, 'Polymorph' and 'Marooned'; from the fourth, 'Dimension Jump' and 'Justice'; from the fifth, 'Back to Reality'; and from the sixth, 'Psirens'. The reason for this apparently random selection is that these were all, at some point, our favourite battle plans.

The army of technicians and artists responsible for making the plan work are too numerous to name individually here, but without their indefatigable contribution we'd just be standing alone in a field somewhere waving a rather limp sword.

This book is dedicated to them.

Grant Naylor, February 1993

BORING TECHNICAL BIT

Wherever possible, we have tried to insert extra technical jargon into the scripts, to confuse and infuriate. See below.

INT.   **INT**erior.

EXT.   **EXT**erior.

OB   Outside Broadcast. (The scene is taped on location, not in the studio.)

PRE-VT   The scene is recorded before the main studio day, usually because it contains special effects that cannot be taped in front of a live audience.

POV   Point Of View. E.g. 'Creature's POV' means the camera sees what the creature sees.

MIX TO   The outgoing shot dissolves into the incoming shot.

VO   Voice Over. (The speaker is not in the shot.)

OOV   Out Of View. (As above.)

SOTTO   Whispered.

SFX   Sound effects.

Special FX   Special effects.

BEAT   Short pause.

DIST   **DIST**orted.

MIC   **MIC**rophone.

POLYMORPH

1. Model shot

Starfield. Strange, ominous music. Slowly a huge pod slides diagonally across screen. On its side we see a skull-and-crossbones logo. Beneath this we read: 'DANGER. GENETIC WASTE. DO NOT OPEN.'

As it glides across the screen we see the metal hull has been ripped open, and whatever was inside has escaped. Suddenly a recorded message crackles into life:

VO:(*As from transmitter*) Danger. Do not attempt to open this pod. The creature inside is extremely hostile. It feeds off the human psyche. It seeks out the deranged, the unbalanced and the emotionally crippled . . .

Cut to:

2. Model shot. Red Dwarf in Space

As we approach the ship, we become aware that a hole has been ripped in the hull.

3. Int. Corridor. Day

POV: CREATURE *on the floor, making curious little noises as it crawls around inspecting things.*

CREATURE: Ho! Huohoh!

It turns the corner. Various bits of mining debris are scattered, including a cracked mirror, which is propped against a wall. Still from the CREATURE's POV, we scuttle along the floor. When we get to the mirror we turn and, for the briefest of brief instants, the CREATURE sees itself in the mirror. It screams, rears up in the air and disappears under a locker. After a beat it emerges.

There is a plip! and the CREATURE transforms itself into a toy truck. Accompanied by a series of plips!, the CREATURE changes into various objects – a soft toy, a vase of flowers – finally ending as a rabbit. The rabbit moves off and plip! – it becomes a beach ball and bounces off down the corridor.

4. Sleeping quarters. Day

LISTER, in a dirty old dressing gown, is preparing for a dinner party. Music in the background. The table has a white surgical gown on it. LISTER lights the two candles, which are stuck in blue plastic bottles. He heads off back to the kitchen section. There is a bowl with minced meat and onions in it, already chopped. He takes a large can of chilli powder and carefully measures out a level teaspoon.

LISTER: Not too little, not too much . . .

He tips the entire can into the bowl and returns the teaspoon to the now empty can. KRYTEN comes in, carrying a vac head and hose. He flips open a groin panel and attaches the vac hose to his groin.

KRYTEN: Just thought I'd give your quarters a quick tickle round, sir. Won't take a jiff.
LISTER: Not now, Kryten – I'm cooking.

KRYTEN twists his left ear, and vacuum-cleaner noise starts up. He vacs round happily.

LISTER: I didn't know you could do that.

KRYTEN *twists his right ear, and the vacuum noise stops.*

KRYTEN: Oh, yes. I can plug a number of add-ons into my groinal socket, allowing me to perform virtually any household task imaginable.

LISTER: Like what?

KRYTEN: You name it: buzz-saw, power drill, hedge-trimmer – even an egg-whisk.

LISTER: What, so you just stick the egg-whisk attachment on the end and you can whip up a Spanish omelette?

KRYTEN: I certainly can, sir. But it's amazing how few people are prepared to eat them.

KRYTEN *twists his left ear, and the vac starts up again. Suddenly his head starts juddering violently, and we hear the sound of a penny jiggling about in a vacuum cleaner. He twists his right ear, and the vacuum stops.*

KRYTEN: My goodness, I must have sucked up a penny. (*Spits one out.*) I'd better change the bag.

He opens up a compartment on his side and removes a full dust bag.

KRYTEN: I'll just get a fresh one.

Exits as the CAT *comes in.*

CAT: Mmmmmm ... Something smells good! What is it? (*Sniffs around.*) It's me! Boy, I love this aftershave!

LISTER: We are five minutes away from the greatest meal of your life, man. Set your taste buds on Def Com Three.

CAT: You've really made an effort here. Where'd you get all this stuff?

LISTER: I just got sick and tired of using plastic knives and forks. So I went down to the medical unit and nicked some gear.

The CAT *picks up a scalpel from his place-setting.*

CAT: This is a scalpel! I'm supposed to cut my food with a scalpel? Something that's been inside someone's guts?

LISTER: It's all been cleaned. It's all been washed and sterilized . . .

CAT: Something that long ago in history may well have performed a certain popular Jewish operation? I'm supposed to eat with this?

LISTER: Get the onion salads out of the fridge.

The CAT goes to the fridge and reads the door.

CAT: 'Embryo refrigeration unit'?

LISTER: How many times? I've cleaned it. It's all clean.

The CAT opens the fridge and looks in.

CAT: Onion salads?

LISTER: In the kidney bowls. Next to the colostomy bag with chilli sauce in it.

The CAT puts two kidney bowls on the table. LISTER opens the microchef door and throws in the minced meat, half a lettuce, a lemon, then squeezes in half a tube of tomato purée and closes the door. He stabs at the control panel. There is a ping. LISTER takes out two plates containing two perfect shami kebabs with elaborately garnished salad.

LISTER: Come on, it's ready. Sit down, sit down.

He puts the two shamis on the table. The CAT sits, picks up his napkin and tucks it into his shirt. LISTER produces a huge syringe.

LISTER: Lemon juice?

CAT: What the hell is that?

LISTER: It's a syringe.

CAT: What kind of a syringe?

LISTER: It's for cows. Artificial insemination. I washed it. It's clean. D'you want lemon juice or what?

The CAT dabs the corners of his mouth with his napkin, throws the napkin across his kebab and gets up.

CAT: What can I say? The whole evening has been totally enchanting, but I've got to go now.

LISTER: What? What about the meal?

CAT: This isn't a meal. It's an autopsy.

LISTER: This is only the starter. What about the main course?

CAT: Hey – you think I've got nothing better to do than hang around watching you serve chicken chausseur in a stool bucket?

The CAT goes.

LISTER: Charming.

LISTER goes over to the fridge.

LISTER: I don't know, you make an effort, you pull out all the stops . . .

Takes out a urine bottle full of red wine.

LISTER: You try to do something with a little bit of extra class . . .

Pours some wine into a bulb-bottom test tube.

LISTER: And where does it get you?

He sips the wine.

LISTER: Hm. Very cheeky.

Suddenly the beach ball bounces into the sleeping quarters. LISTER catches it and puts it on the table. Puzzled, he goes to the hatchway and looks out.

5. Int. Long, empty corridor. Day

LISTER *peeps out. Nobody there.*

6. Int. Sleeping quarters. Day

LISTER *sits back down at the table. The ball's not there.* LISTER *looks under the table. As he does so, we see there are now three kebabs on his plate.*

7. Pre-record. Home movie in forest. Day

Full screen. This is a Rimmer home movie. A tablecloth is spread on the grass, and four boys and a woman are having a picnic. No sound. Pull out. We see this is being projected on to a large monitor in:

8. Int. Science Room. Day

RIMMER *is watching, smiling.* KRYTEN *comes in, carrying the vac head and hose.*

KRYTEN: Ah! Sorry to interrupt . . . I, uh . . . just need to get a . . . sorry.
RIMMER: No, no, Kryten. It's all right. Just running a few of the old home movies. That's me. There're my brothers, John, Frank and Howard. God, we were close. The Four Musketeers we used to call ourselves. Well, the Three Musketeers, actually: but they always let me be the Queen of Spain . . . marvellous.

On the monitor: the picnic is over. One of the boys is being staked out on the grass by the other three. Guess who. They smear jam over his struggling pasty-white frame. The oldest of the boys produces a can, which he holds up to the camera. A crudely hand-written label says: 'Ants'. He takes the top off the can and pours sultanas over the near-hysterical young RIMMER.

RIMMER: Yes, I was the butt of the occasional practical joke but nothing sinister. Just the usual boyhood pranks, you know: apple-pie beds, black-eye telescopes. One time they even hid a small land mine in my sandpit . . . took it from my father's gun cabinet. I mean, how were they supposed to know it was going to go off? Marvellous guys.

There is a close-up of the woman – mid-fifties, stern-looking.

KRYTEN: An old girlfriend, Mr Arnold, sir?

RIMMER: (*Raises eyebrow*) Hardly.

KRYTEN: No, no. Not really your type, I suppose. Silly old trout like that.

RIMMER: She's my mother.

KRYTEN: Oh, sir, I'm so sorry . . . How could I say that?

RIMMER: Forget it.

KRYTEN: How can I forget it? I compared your mother to a foolish, aged, blubbery fish. I said she was a scaly old piscine! I intimated she was an ugly, lungless marine animal with galloping senility. A putrid, amphibious gill-breather with less brains than a mollusc.

RIMMER: Look at her. Magnificent woman! Very prim, very proper, almost austere. Some people took her for cold, thought she was aloof. Not a bit of it. She just despised fools. Quite tragic, really, because otherwise I think we'd have got on famously. Ah, well.

KRYTEN: If you'll excuse me, sir: clearly this is a very private family moment. I, uh . . . I've no fish to embarrass you any further. I'll let myself trout.

KRYTEN leaves. Pause. Comes back in again.

KRYTEN: (*Guilty*) Oh, sir . . .

RIMMER: Just go.

KRYTEN leaves. HOLLY has appeared on the monitor screen.

HOLLY: I don't want you to panic, Arn, but it does appear that there is a very tiny possibility that, in fact, there may very well, in all likelihood, possibly, be a non-human life form on board.

RIMMER: You mean like last time? When you got us all

worked up, and we went scooting down to the cargo bay, complete with bazookoids and backpacks? And it turned out to be one of Lister's socks?

HOLLY: Well, I didn't recognize the genetic structure. Biologically speaking, they were a completely new life form.

RIMMER: Absolutely ridiculous. I felt a total goit.

HOLLY: Well, I think you should take a butcher's.

RIMMER: Where is it?

HOLLY: I lost it somewhere along the Habitation Decks.

9. Int. Sleeping quarters. Day

LISTER *has eaten two of his kebabs. The third one remains.* KRYTEN *comes in.*

KRYTEN: Enjoying your meal, sir?

LISTER: De-smegging-licious. It's my own recipe. Shami Kebab Diabolo. It's beautiful, man, like eating molten lava.

He wipes the sweat from his brow, and takes a swig of Leopard lager.

LISTER: I cooked one for Petersen once. He was in sick bay for a week. Weed.

KRYTEN *starts attaching the vac hose to his groin.* LISTER *turns back to start his kebab. He pours salt on it. The kebab sneezes.* LISTER *squeezes lemon on to it.*

KEBAB: (*Disgusted*) Ho-o-ooo!

LISTER: (*To* KRYTEN) What did you say?

KRYTEN: I didn't say anything, sir.

LISTER *leans forward to sniff the kebab. He prods the kebab gently with his fork. It growls at him.* LISTER *starts to back off. The kebab launches itself at his throat.* LISTER *falls backwards off his chair and hurls himself around the sleeping quarters, trying to pull the kebab off his throat. He gives a throttled cry.* KRYTEN *looks down at him and shakes his head.*

KRYTEN: You seriously like them that hot?
LISTER: (*Strangulated*) Help muhhh!

LISTER *thrashes around on the floor.*

LISTER: The kebab – it's trying to kill me!
KRYTEN: Oh, it's a good one, huh?

LISTER *wrestles the kebab from his throat, grabs a baseball bat and starts hammering the killer kebab – mostly missing. The kebab scuttles under a locker. We hear the familiar* plip! LISTER *sticks his baseball bat under the locker and starts banging it around.*

LISTER: There's something there – I can see it! Throw me that torch.

KRYTEN *throws him a torch.*

KRYTEN: Are you quite all right, sir?

LISTER *fishes out a pair of boxer shorts.*

LISTER: Smeg. It's gone.

He picks up the boxers and starts looking around the sleeping quarters.

LISTER: How can that be? Where's it gone?

He starts pulling on the boxers under his dressing gown.

LISTER: Come on, Kryten – let's get out of here. Something very weird is happening. Something very . . . (*Winces.*)
KRYTEN: What?

From under Lister's dressing gown we hear:

CREATURE: Ho!
LISTER: Just a pain in my groin. Come on, we've got to get . . . ah!
CREATURE: Ho!
KRYTEN: Sir?

LISTER: Agh!

KRYTEN: What's wrong?

LISTER: My ... ah! ... My boxers ... aaah! ... They're shrinking.

There is a cracking sound as the underpants contract.

LISTER: My underpants! They're alive! And they're getting smaller ... ahhhhhh! No, God! Please! Please!

He throws himself about the sleeping quarters, across the table, and falls at Kryten's feet. RIMMER *walks in and stands at the door.*

LISTER: Kryten – help me! Please help me ... My boxers – take them off! Pull them down! Quick – I'm begging you!

KRYTEN *bends to help him, his groinal hose still securely attached.*

KRYTEN: Keep still, Mr David ...

LISTER: I can't stand it any more! Get them off! Please!

KRYTEN: Keep still!

LISTER: This is torture! Pull them down!

KRYTEN *finally yanks them off. The boxers have shrunk to three-year-old size. He tosses them away.*

RIMMER: Well. I can't say I'm totally shocked. I wish I could, but I can't.

LISTER *staggers painfully to his bunk.*

RIMMER: You'll bonk anything, won't you, Lister! Not even an android's safe from your vile appetites.

LISTER: The boxers – where are they?

KRYTEN: I threw them over here ... They've gone.

LISTER: Are you sure?

KRYTEN: (*Examining Lister's bunk*) There's nothing here – just the blankets and the pillow and the snake.

KRYTEN *holds up a large snake, and continues looking through the bunk.*

RIMMER: Snake!
LISTER: Snake!

KRYTEN *looks at it, realizes for the first time and yells.*

KRYTEN: Snake!!

He throws the snake across the room indiscriminately. It lands on Lister. He catches it and, with a cry of horror, throws it in the laundry basket and jams the lid on top.

RIMMER: What the smeg is going on?
LISTER: My god, my god, my god. I hate snakes.

One hand on the lid, he fiddles around in the tray of surgical instruments and finds a long, sharp, dangerous-looking one.

LISTER: They freak me out, totally. Snakes! Yeuch! They're
   my second all-time worst fear.
RIMMER: What's your first?

LISTER *whips off the laundry-basket lid, brandishing his weapon. The most disgusting creature — an enormous set of jaws on an armour-plated head, slobbering unspeakable mucal secretions — looms hugely out of the basket and lets out a stomach-churning roar.* LISTER *stands quivering and points.*

LISTER: This!

Suddenly a tentacle shoots out of its mouth and sticks to Lister's forehead. LISTER *and the* CREATURE *both glow red, and there's a sucking sound — as if the Creature is draining something from Lister.* LISTER *collapses.*

10. Int. Science Room. Day

LISTER *is on a medical table.* KRYTEN *is looking at bio-feedback computers.*

CAT: Is he OK?

RIMMER: As far as we can tell, yes.

CAT: So, where'd it go?

RIMMER: It turned into some sort of splodgy, squelchy thing and squidged off down the corridor.

CAT: What is it? Some kind of alien?

HOLLY: No – it's from Earth. Man-made. I checked out its DNA profile. It's some kind of genetic experiment that went wrong.

KRYTEN: Apparently, it was an attempt to create the Ultimate Warrior. A mutant that could change shape to suit its terrain and deceive its enemies.

CAT: So, what went wrong?

KRYTEN: It's insane.

LISTER *starts to wake.*

HOLLY: It feeds off negative emotions: fear, guilt, anger, paranoia. Drains them out of its prey.

KRYTEN: It's a sort of emotional vampire. It changes shape to provoke a negative emotion – in Lister's case, it took him to the very limit of his terror, then sucked out his fear.

RIMMER: So Lister's got no sense of fear now?

KRYTEN: Precisely.

RIMMER: So, what are we going to do?

LISTER: Well, I say let's get out there and twat it!

RIMMER: Lister, you're ill. Just relax and leave this to us.

LISTER: I could have had it in the sleeping quarters, but you saw it, you saw it: it took me by surprise.

RIMMER: Lister – it turned into an eight-foot-tall, armour-plated alien killing machine.

LISTER: If it wants a barny, we'll give it one. One swift knee in its happy sacs, it'll drop, like anyone else.

RIMMER: Fine, well, we'll certainly bear that in mind when we're constructing our strategy.

LISTER: I'll rip out its windpipe and beat it to death with the tonsil end!

RIMMER: Yes. Very good.

LISTER: I'll shove my fist so far down its throat, I'll be able to pull the label off its underpants.

KRYTEN *injects* LISTER *with sedative.*

LISTER: What's that, pal? You starting trouble?

KRYTEN: Just a little something to calm you down, sir.

LISTER: Come on, then! All of you slags! I'll have you all. Who's first? One at a time or all together. Makes no odds to me. I'll . . . I'll . . .

LISTER *slumps into unconsciousness.*

RIMMER: All right. As far as I can see, we've got two options: One, take it on and kill it or, two, run away. Who's for two?

KRYTEN: Two sounds pretty good to me, sir.

CAT: Always been my lucky number.

KRYTEN: I'll load up Starbug.

HOLLY: What about Lister?

RIMMER: Seal the hatch from the inside. He'll be safe here till we're ready to go. Let's move.

KRYTEN: What about the Space Corps directive, which states that it's our primary, overriding duty to contact other life forms, exchange information and, wherever possible, bring them home?

RIMMER: What about the Rimmer directive, which states: never tangle with anything that's got more teeth than the entire Osmond family.

11. Int. Lift. Night
A wire cage lift, descending creakily. Eerie atmos. CAT *and* KRYTEN *are both clutching bazookoids.* KRYTEN *is holding a psi-scan.*

12. Int. Warehouse. Night
They get out of the lift and prowl along. The psi-scan emits a regular beep. Suddenly it starts beeping rapidly.

KRYTEN: It's here!

CAT: Where?!

KRYTEN: Somewhere.

RIMMER: Set the bazookoids to heat-seeker. When we see it, just aim roughly in its direction and the heat-seekers'll do the rest.

KRYTEN *and* CAT *switch the bazookoids. They walk down an aisle of packing crates.*

RIMMER: There! In the shadows! There!

CAT *and* KRYTEN *fire off a volley, and two laser bolts scream down the length of the warehouse.*

RIMMER: Sorry, my fault. False alarm.

CAT: Idiot.

Shot: the laser bolts reach the end of the warehouse, flip over and start powering towards them. They dive out of the way, and the bolts zip over them.

RIMMER: I don't understand it. A hologram doesn't produce heat and neither does an android. What are they homing in on?

RIMMER *and* KRYTEN *look at the Cat.*

CAT: So long, guys.

The CAT *gets up and races round a corner. The laser bolts zoom back and follow him.*

13. Int. Warehouse. Night

The CAT *ducks into a recess in the crates. The lasers zip past him. He looks out. The bolts turn and head back towards him.*

CAT: Oh, gimme a break!

He runs off, zig-zagging through the crate matrix. He finally believes he's shaken them. He strolls round a corner, and they're both hovering in the air. He runs down a crate alley. Both the laser bolts are almost on him. He reaches a door, opens it and ducks. Both bolts zoom over his head and through. The CAT *slams it shut and locks them in. He peers through the three-inch-square viewing window in the door, where the bolts are hovering, thwarted.*

CAT: You either got it or you ain't. And, boys, you ain't even close.

In the distance, we hear:

RIMMER: (*VO*) Cat? Where are you?
CAT: Over here.

14. Int. Warehouse. Night

RIMMER *and* KRYTEN.

RIMMER: Stay put. We'll come and find you.
KRYTEN: Keep talking.

15. Int. Warehouse. Night

The CAT *creeps to the end of a row of packing cases and turns. He looks down the aisle. It's empty. A beautiful* WOMAN *in slinky evening clothes leans over his shoulder.*

WOMAN: What are you looking for?
CAT: A mutant. It's dangerous. It can turn into anything.
WOMAN: It sounds pretty scary.
CAT: It is, baby, believe me.

They move off.

WOMAN: It must take a brave kind of guy to do this kind of work.
CAT: Guess you're right.
WOMAN: And smart. Bet you have to be smart.

CAT: Smart? Yeah, you definitely have to be smart. Like I say, it can turn into anything. You've got to have your wits about you all the time. Don't let up for one second. Or it'll just creep up on you and, *plip!*, you're dog meat.

WOMAN: You're quite a guy. Brave. Smart. Handsome.

CAT: You think handsome?

WOMAN: Oh, come on – you're probably the best-looking guy I've ever seen.

CAT: Well, I wasn't going to be the first to say it . . .

WOMAN: You know what I would really like? I would really like to make love to a guy like you.

CAT: Well, I'm sure I have a window in my schedule somewhere. Let's see, what are you doing in, say, ten seconds' time?

WOMAN: Nothing I couldn't cancel.

CAT: Hi, I'm the Cat.

WOMAN: Hi. I'm the genetic mutant.

CAT: Glad to know you. Genny who?

The CAT does a double-take. There is a plip! *sound. When we cut back to the WOMAN, she is now the beast from the laundry basket. The draining tentacle zips out and sticks on the CAT's forehead. They both glow red, and there is the draining/sucking sound.*

16. Int. Warehouse. Night

KRYTEN *and* RIMMER *running.* KRYTEN *in the lead.*

RIMMER: It's got him! It's got him!

17. Int. Warehouse. Night

CAT, *unconscious on the floor.* KRYTEN *races up to him.*

KRYTEN: My goodness! Are you all right?

As KRYTEN *kneels and passes his psi-scan over the Cat,* RIMMER *comes up behind.*

16

RIMMER: Is he dead?

KRYTEN: Unconscious. But, according to the psi-scan, he appears to have lost an emotion.

RIMMER: Which emotion?

KRYTEN: He's lost his vanity.

RIMMER: This is your fault, Kryten.

KRYTEN: Muh-my fault?

RIMMER: We were supposed to stick together — you let the Cat run off alone.

KRYTEN: But that wasn't . . . I mean . . .

RIMMER: He trusted you. And look at him now.

KRYTEN *absolutely racked with guilt.*

KRYTEN: Oh, please . . . I feel so . . . so . . .

RIMMER: (*Hisses*) Guil-teeee!

KRYTEN: Yes!

RIMMER: Good!

RIMMER *grins. His head distorts as he transforms into the armour-plated beast. The suction tentacle lands on Kryten's forehead. The real* RIMMER *dashes round the corner. He freezes as he sees the* MUTANT *bent over Kryten. He shudders in disgust and then tries to think of something to do.*

RIMMER: Shoo!

Plip! *The* MUTANT *turns into the squelchy crabby thing and scuttles off.* RIMMER *runs up to Kryten.*

RIMMER: Let's get Lister and get out of here.

KRYTEN: It's got my guilt. I have lost the single emotion which prevents my transgressing the norms, mores and manners of civilized society.

RIMMER: Come on, let's go.

KRYTEN: Screw you, Hadron Head!

18. Int. Science Room. Night

We start on the profile of a sink with a dripping tap. LISTER *is sleeping on the medical bed in the background. There is a creaking noise, like expanding metal. Before our eyes, the tap begins to bulge. It bulges and bulges and then out pops a miniature version of the Polymorph. It squiggles across the floor to Lister's bed.*

19. Int. Corridor. Night

Empty corridor. Off, we hear:

RIMMER: Come on! Hurry up! Let's go!

RIMMER *rounds the corner alone and turns to speak to the other two. Still out of shot.*

RIMMER: Come on!

The CAT *staggers round the corner. He looks like Fat Freddy of the Furry Freak Brothers – dirty, unkempt. He's clutching a bottle of something in a brown paper bag.*

CAT: I've been getting myself comfortable, man.

He belches in Rimmer's face.

RIMMER: Kryten – come on! You're holding us all up!
KRYTEN Who cares?
RIMMER: You'll get us all killed!
KRYTEN: So?

KRYTEN *cuffs the back of the Cat's head and walks on. The* CAT *swigs from his bottle and belches again.*

20. Int. Science Room. Night

LISTER *is in the medical bed with a fifty-five-year-old* WOMAN *in a flannelette nightie. He's dozing; she's stroking his chest.* RIMMER *comes in with* KRYTEN *and the* CAT.

KRYTEN: Oh look, it's Bonehead's mother.

RIMMER: Mother?

MRS RIMMER: Hello, dear.

RIMMER: What are you doing?

MRS RIMMER: What does it look like, darling?

RIMMER: You've just made love to my mother??!

HOLLY: It's not your mother. It's the Polymorph.

RIMMER: You've just had my mum?

MRS RIMMER: Five times! He was like a wild stallion!

KRYTEN: (*Laughing*) Very prim, very proper – almost austere.

HOLLY: Don't fall for it, Arn. It's trying to make you angry.

MRS RIMMER: Oh, darling, I wish you could have seen him in action – he was like a set of pistons in an ocean liner's engine room.

HOLLY: Don't get angry . . . That's what it wants . . .

RIMMER: (*Through clenched teeth*) Lister and mother – it's a dream come true!

MRS RIMMER: So energetic. At one point, I honestly thought my false teeth were going to fall out.

RIMMER: (*Struggling to keep control*) How lovely.

MRS RIMMER: And, Arnold, the things this boy can do with alphabetti spaghetti!

RIMMER: (*Finally blows*) Alphabetti spaghetti?!?!?

A tentacle shoots out and sticks on his head. The red glow, the sucking noise.

21. Model shot. Red Dwarf in Space

22. Int. Sleeping quarters. Night

LISTER *is sitting on the bunk, checking out his bazookoid.* RIMMER *is sitting cross-legged on the table, with a little goatee beard, an unlit pipe and a tee shirt bearing the legend 'Give quiche a chance'. The* CAT *is cowering under the table.* KRYTEN *is pacing.*

19

CAT: Where is it now?

HOLLY: It's gone back down to the cargo bays. Sleeping off a four-course meal of fear, vanity, guilt and anger. You've got to get it before it comes back for seconds.

RIMMER: Look: just because it's an armour-plated alien killing machine that salivates unspeakable slobber doesn't mean it's a bad person. What we've got to do is get it round a table and put together a solution package, probably over tea and biscuits.

KRYTEN: We can't trust his opinion – he's got no anger. He's a total dork!

RIMMER: Good point, Kryten. Let's take that on board, shall we? David, do you have anything you want to bring to this forum?

LISTER: Well, yes, I have, actually, Arnold. Why don't we go down to the ammunition store, get the nuclear warheads, then strap one to my head, and I'll nut the smegger into oblivion. Ka-boooom!

RIMMER: Right, well, that's very nice, David. Let's put that one on the back burner, shall we? Cat, let's have your contribution. Come on.

CAT: (*Mumbles drunkenly*) Well, don't ask me my opinion. I'm nobody. Just pretend I'm not here.

RIMMER: That's lovely. Thank you very much. Moving on a step . . . and I hope no one thinks I'm setting myself up as a self-elected chairperson: just see me as a facilitator. Uh, Kryten. What's your view? Don't be shy.

KRYTEN: Well, I think we should send Lister in as a decoy. Then, while it's busy eating him alive, we can creep up on it unawares and blast it into the stratosphere.

LISTER: Good plan. That's the best plan yet. Let it get knackered eating me to death, and you guys take it un-awares.

RIMMER: Well, that's certainly an option, David, yes. But here's my proposal . . . Let's get tough. The time for talking is over. Now, call it extreme if you like, but I propose we hit it hard, and hit it fast, with a major, and I mean *major*, leaflet campaign. And, while it's reeling from that, we follow up with a whist drive, a car-boot sale and possibly even some benefit concerts. OK? Now, if that's not enough, then, sorry, it's time for the tee shirts: 'MUTANTS OUT', 'CHAMELEONIC LIFE FORMS – NO THANKS'. And if that's not enough, well, I don't know what will be.

KRYTEN: Has anyone ever told you that you are a disgusting pus-filled bubo who has all the wit, charm and self-possession of an Alsatian dog after a head-swap operation?

LISTER: Listen, you bunch of tarts: it's clobberin' time. There's a body bag out there with that scud-ball's name on it, and I'm doing up the zip. Anyone who gets in my way gets a napalm enema.

CAT: Well, I think everyone's right. Except me. So just forget I spoke.

RIMMER: I think we're all beginning to lose sight of the real issue here, which is what we are going to call ourselves. And I think it comes down to a choice between the League Against Salivating Monsters or my own personal preference, which is the Committee for the Liberation and Integration of Terrifying Organisms and their Rehabilitation Into Society. Uh, one drawback with that: the abbreviation spells Clitoris.

LISTER: Look – it needs killing, and if that means I have to sacrifice my life in some stupid pointless way, I'm all for it.

KRYTEN: Yes, why not? Even if it doesn't work, at least it'll be a laugh.

LISTER: Right! So let's cut all of this business and get on with it. Last one alive's a wet ponce. Who's with me?

RIMMER: Well, the car stickers aren't ready till Thursday, but sometimes one just has to act spontaneously. People – let's go.

CAT: I'm coming. Maybe I can bum some money from him.
KRYTEN: Maybe if I hand you guys over, he'll let me go. (*Trains bazookoid on the Cat.*) Move it, suckers!

23. Int. Warehouse. Night

LISTER, *armed to the teeth — bazookoid, gun belts, knife in the mouth. Next to him* RIMMER *is carrying a hologramatic placard,* 'MUTANT — WE LOVE YOU', *humming happily. The* CAT, *even more bedraggled, follows behind, swigging from a bottle of whisky. At the rear,* KRYTEN *is prodding them along, bazookoid in hand.*

KRYTEN: Here, mutie mutant!
LISTER: Where are you, you chicken? Show us your slobbery chops, and I'll blow 'em off.
KRYTEN: They're here! Come and get them! Nice, juicy humans.
CAT: It's not here. (*Burps.*)
KRYTEN: Let's try the next level.

They walk down an aisle of crates towards a door. We are vaguely aware we've been here before. Suddenly, behind them, the POLY-MORPH *looms up in all its saliva-slobbering glory. The* CAT *opens the door, and we see the two laser bolts from earlier on are hovering, ready for the kill. Everyone ducks. The bolts shoot over their heads, and the* POLYMORPH *explodes into a gazillion splodgy fragments. Coloured lights swoosh around, and, with a whooshing noise, their emotions are returned to them. They stagger about, recovering.*

CAT: What am I wearing? I smell like a dinosaur's jockey shorts!
KRYTEN: Sirs, naturally I will commit suicide immediately.

KRYTEN *raises his bazookoid to his mouth.* LISTER *bats it away.*

LISTER: Hey — we were all a bit whacked out, there.
RIMMER: You can say that again.

22

CAT: Come on. Let's go and clean up. If I don't get into some co-ordinated evening wear, I'm gonna have to resign my post as Most Handsome Guy on the Ship!

24. Model shot. Red Dwarf in Space

25. Model shot. The Pod

We see the inscription on the side: 'DANGER. GENETIC WASTE. DO NOT OPEN.' And, below the rip in the metal, the inscription: 'CONTENTS: 2'.

26. Int. Corridor. Night

Wearily, they each tramp across frame. First, LISTER. *Second,* KRYTEN. *Third,* RIMMER. *Fourth,* CAT. *Fifth,* LISTER *again. The final* LISTER *looks at the camera. His head spins while his body remains static. He grins at the camera, then walks off.*

MAROONED

1. Model shot. Cargo bay

Starbug *stands in the cargo bay. Red alert lights flash, and a siren is wailing.*

HOLLY: Abandon ship! Black Hole approaching. Abandon ship . . .

The siren stops.

HOLLY: Oh, god, now the siren's broken. Awooga, awooga. Abandon ship . . .

2. Int. Starbug cockpit. Day

Throughout the scene, a red light is flashing. HOLLY *is on a monitor.*

RIMMER: But a Black Hole's a huge, compacted star! It's millions of miles wide. Why didn't you see it on the radar screen?

HOLLY: Well, the thing about *a* Black Hole – its main distinguishing feature – is it's black. And the thing about space, your basic space colour is black. So how are you s'posed to see them?

RIMMER: But five of them! How can you be ambushed by five Black Holes?

HOLLY: Always the way, isn't it? You hang around in Deep Space for three million years and you don't see one. Then, all of a sudden, five all turn up at once.

3. Int. Starbug rear. Day

KRYTEN *and* LISTER *enter carrying an ornate trunk.* LISTER *has his guitar slung over his shoulder.*

LISTER: Come on – we've got less than twenty minutes.

RIMMER: Careful . . . careful . . . Mind the hatchway! Don't knock it!

LISTER: What d'you want to bring this piece of junk for?

RIMMER: That 'piece of junk' happens to be a Javanese camphor-wood chest. It belonged to my father. It's got all my valuables in it.

KRYTEN *goes out.* LISTER *opens the trunk and peers inside.*

LISTER: I never realized you had so much crap. What's this?

Brings up handful of fairly hefty wooden soldiers.

LISTER: Toy soldiers?

RIMMER: Toy soldiers? (*Laughs.*) They've been in our family for years. They're priceless nineteenth-century replicas of Napoleon's Armée du Nord.

LISTER *turns the soldiers over in his hand.*

LISTER: So you can't change the clothes and that, like you can with Sindy?

LISTER *places the soldiers back in the box. Spots something else.*

LISTER: And what the smeg's this?

LISTER *pulls out several wads of bank notes.*

RIMMER: Just what little I've managed to scrimp and scrape, by tossing the odd copper aside for a rainy day.

LISTER: There must be twenty grand here.

RIMMER: Twenty-four. Look – I thought we were supposed to be getting off the ship.

LISTER *and* RIMMER *step up into:*

4. Int. Starbug cockpit. Day

LISTER: Twenty-four thousand!? And you had the front to borrow money off me to buy me a birthday present?

RIMMER: It was only fifteen quid.

LISTER: Right. Fifteen quid. And what did I get? A five-quid book token.

RIMMER: Those cards aren't free, you know. I had to fork out for that as well.

LISTER: And you never paid me back. You're tighter than an Italian waiter's keks.

The CAT *and* KRYTEN *come in.*

KRYTEN: Blue Midget is loaded.

RIMMER: Are you sure you've got everything?

KRYTEN: Just the bare essentials – food and medical supplies.

CAT: Yeah, I'm just taking the bare essentials, too – thirty-six changes of clothing and ten full-length dress mirrors.

LISTER: Cat – we're going to be away twelve hours.

CAT: You think I need more mirrors?

LISTER: Come on, let's move it.

5. Model shot. Starbug and Blue Midget leave Red Dwarf and split off

Over, we hear:

HOLLY: OK, this is the plan: I'll try and navigate Red Dwarf through the minefield of Black Holes. If all goes well, we'll all rendezvous on the desert moon Sigma four D.

CAT: What happens if all doesn't go well?

HOLLY: Well, Red Dwarf and everything in it will be compacted to the size of a small garden pea.

CAT: Bye bye, Birdseye.

6. Int. Starbug rear. Day

The control consoles all read 'autopilot'. LISTER *is at the table, eating a curry, turning one of Rimmer's toy soldiers over in his other hand.*

RIMMER: Look, please, honestly. They're priceless.

LISTER: I'm just having a goosie.

RIMMER: Look, if you get curry all over them, how's that going to look? What's Lieutenant-General Baron Jaquinaux of the First Cavalry Division supposed to be doing with meat vindaloo all over his tunic?

LISTER: It'll make him look more authentic. People'll think he's got dysentery.

LISTER *puts them back in the trunk.*

LISTER: You're obsessed with war, aren't you? You collect toy soldiers, play war games, read all those stupid combat mags. And half your books are on Patton and Caesar and various other gits.

RIMMER: It's about leadership. That's what I admire — the ability to command, to out-think a worthy opponent on the field of battle.

LISTER: It's just so ironic, when deep down you're such a basic, natural coward.

RIMMER: Coward?

LISTER: Planet leave, Miranda? That space bar, the 'Hacienda'? When that fight started up? You were out of that door quicker than a whippet with a bumful of dynamite!

RIMMER: That was a bar-room brawl! A common pub fight. A shambolic, drunken set-to.

LISTER: Which you started.

RIMMER: I just made an innocuous comment, I merely voiced a rumour that MacWilliams was sexually tilted in favour of sleeping with the dead. I didn't start the rumour. I simply voiced it.

LISTER: To his face. Right to his face. When he was with his four biggest mates. Then you did your Roadrunner act, and left me to face the music.

RIMMER: I could have got hurt.

LISTER: You'd have made a brilliant general, wouldn't you?

RIMMER: Generals don't smash chairs over people's heads. They don't smash Newcastle Brown bottles into your face and say, 'Stitch that, Jimmy.' They're in the nice white tent on top of the hill, sipping Sancerre and directing the battle. They're Men of Honour.

LISTER: I don't believe it! You make war sound romantic.

RIMMER: I'll tell you something. Something I've never told anyone. When I was fifteen, I went to Macedonia on a school trip, to the site of Alexander the Great's palace. And for the first time in my whole life, I felt . . . I felt I was home. This palace was where I belonged. Years later, I got friendly with a hypnotherapist – Donald – and told him about the Alexander the Great thing, and he said he'd regress me back through my past lives. I was dubious, but I let him put me under. It turned out my instincts were absolutely correct – I had lived a past life in Macedonia. That palace was my home. Because, believe it or not, Lister, he told me that, in a previous incarnation, I was Alexander the Great's chief eunuch.

LISTER: Do you know something? I believe you.

RIMMER: He didn't say I was Alexander himself, which is obviously what I wanted to hear. But it explained everything: I'd lived a previous life alongside one of the greatest generals in history. No wonder the military's in my blood.

LISTER: No wonder you're such a good singer.

RIMMER: Well, maybe it's rot, I don't know. But it's funny – to this day, I can't look at a pair of nutcrackers without wincing. And why is it, whenever I'm with a large group of women, I have this overwhelming urge to bathe them all in warm olive oil?

LISTER: I have that urge, Rimmer. It's got nothing to do with past lives.

RIMMER: Well, why is it, then?

LISTER *steps up into the cockpit. Stars glint through the front-view window behind him.*

LISTER: It's because you're unhappy with your own weasly, humdrum existence. You're looking for something with a bit more . . . I don't know . . . glamour.

Behind him, we see a flaming meteor hurtling towards them. RIMMER'S *eyes widen slightly as panic robs him of the power of speech.*

LISTER: Now is what counts – you've got to live life today. Who knows what's going to happen tomorrow? Who knows what's going to happen in the next five minutes? That's what makes life so exciting.

The meteor smashes into them.

7. Model shot
Meteor collides with Starbug, *sending it spinning into the atmosphere of the moon below.*

8. Model shot
Starbug *overheating as it plummets through cloud.*

9. Model shot
Starbug *crash-lands on snowy landscape and screams to a halt.*

LISTER: (*VO*) You see what I mean?

10. Stock footage. Arctic wasteland
Blizzard. Mix to:

11. Model shot
Starbug *in snowy wasteland.*

12. Ext. Starbug crashed
Starbug's *door opens (the rest of what we can see of the vehicle is covered in snow).* LISTER, *wearing a huge, furry anorak, a shovel strapped to his back, opens the door and fights against the wind and the blizzard to get out. He manages to open it far enough to get his head out, then the door snaps back, and Lister's face is shut in the door, contorted out of shape. He finally manages to push it open and falls out of shot. We see him holding on to the craft, fighting against the incredibly strong wind, edging his way gingerly to the front. As he lets go of the ship to unhook his shovel, he gets blown away. He's yanked completely out of shot.*

We then see him being dragged along the ground on his back, finally smashing to rest against an ice dune.

We cut to: LISTER *crawling on his knees against the wind, using his shovel like a canoe paddle.*

Cut to: LISTER *tying a rope around his waist, then tying it to the craft. He tugs the rope and tests it. When he feels safe enough, he reaches back for his shovel. With a snap, the rope breaks, and he gets yanked out of frame again.*

13. Int. Starbug rear. Night
RIMMER *is leaning over the controls. A monitor screen is buzzing with interference.*

RIMMER: Mayday! Mayday! Can you read me? Come in, please. Can you read me?

The outer door opens, and LISTER *stumbles in, followed by a blizzard. He stands shivering.*

RIMMER: (*Without looking up*) Still snowing, is it?

LISTER *sits at the table.*

LISTER: It's useless. You can hardly stand up, never mind dig it out. No luck?

RIMMER: Nothing's getting through.

LISTER: Three days! They must be looking for us by now Where the smeg are they?

RIMMER: It's impossible to find us in this weather. They could be ten feet away and walk straight past us

LISTER: We're going to die, aren't we? How much food is there?

RIMMER: There's half a bag of soggy Smoky Bacon Crisps, a tin of mustard powder, a brown lemon, three water biscuits, two bottles of vinegar and a tube of Bonjella gum ointment.

LISTER: Gum ointment?

RIMMER: Yes, it was in the first-aid box. It's that minty flavour. It's quite nice.

LISTER: It's quite nice if you smear it on your mouth ulcer, but you can't sit down and eat it.

RIMMER: You may have to.

LISTER: That's it? There's nothing else?

RIMMER: Just a Pot Noodle. Oh, and I found a tin of dog food in the tool cupboard.

LISTER: (Sighs) Well. Pretty obvious what gets eaten last. I can't stand Pot Noodles. (Pause.) We're going to die, aren't we? Correction – I'm going to die. You're a hologram. You're already dead. You don't need food.

RIMMER: Did you find any wood?

LISTER: There's no wood. There's no vegetation out there. Smeg all. Just a wasteland.

RIMMER: We can't let that fire go out – it's your only form of heat.

LISTER: I'm going to die, aren't I? God, I'm hungry. I'm going to have the crisps . . .

RIMMER: No!

LISTER: Just one.

RIMMER: You ate less than sixteen hours ago.

LISTER: It's all right for you. You don't even feel the cold.

RIMMER: Take your mind off it. Find something to put on the fire.

LISTER *gets up and starts to look for something to burn.*

RIMMER: Mayday! Mayday! (*To Lister*) I wonder why it's 'Mayday'?

LISTER *gathers some books from the trunk.*

LISTER: Eh?

RIMMER: The distress call. Why d'you say 'Mayday'? It's only a Bank Holiday. Why not 'Shrove Tuesday', or 'Ascension Sunday'? (*Mimics*) Ascension Sunday! Ascension Sunday! The fifteenth Wednesday after Pentecost! The fifteenth Wednesday after Pentecost!

LISTER: It's French, you doink. It's *m'aidez*. Help me. Muh-aid-ay (*Sighs.*) Everywhere I look reminds me of food. Look at these books: Charles Lamb, Herman Wok, the complete works of Sir Francis Bacon, Eric Van Lustbader . . .

RIMMER: Eric Van Lustbader? What's he got to do with food?

LISTER: *Van*. Bread van, meat van, food!

RIMMER: Look, you're getting obsessed.

LISTER: It's these books! It's like someone's put them here to taunt me. Look at this – *The Caretaker* by Harold Pinta.

RIMMER: It's 'Pinter'. Stop thinking about food.

LISTER: Take my mind off it. Talk about something.

RIMMER: Like what?

LISTER: Anything.

RIMMER: Urmmmm . . .

LISTER: Come on!

RIMMER: Anything apart from food?

LISTER: Don't talk about food!

RIMMER: I just can't think of another topic.

LISTER: Don't mention topics! They're food! Tell me **a** story. Any story.

RIMMER: I don't know any stories.

LISTER: Anything. Tell me how you lost your virginity.

RIMMER: My what?

LISTER: Come on. Talk to me.

RIMMER: How I lost it? Well it was so long ago ... I was so young and sexually precocious, I'm not sure I can remember.

LISTER: Everyone can remember how they lost their virginity. It's one of those things ... like everyone can remember where they were the day Cliff Richard was shot. Or when the first woman landed on Pluto. Or when they installed the gigantic toupee over the Earth to cover the gap in the ozone layer. It's just one of those things you always remember.

RIMMER: Well, I don't. Good grief, you can hardly expect me to recall every single sexual liaison I've ever partaken of. What d'you think I am – Marvo the Memory Man?

LISTER: Come on, Rimmer. The truth.

RIMMER: The truth? Not much to tell, really. I've always been a bit of a fish out of water when it comes to women. Never know what to say. I wasn't very highly sexed, to be honest with you. I think it was all that school cabbage I was forced to eat as a boy. Still, the first-ever time ... the first time was this girl I met at Cadet College. Sandra, she was called. We did it in the back of my brother's car.

LISTER: What was it like?

RIMMER: Oh, brilliant. Incredible. (*Goes glassy-eyed.*) Bentley convertible. V8 turbo. Walnut burr panelling. Marvellous machine. So what about you?

LISTER: Michelle Fisher. The ninth hole of Bootle Municipal golf course. Par four, dogleg to the right, in the bunker behind the green.

RIMMER: You lost your virginity on a golf course? How did you have the nerve?

LISTER: It wasn't in the middle of the Ryder Cup or anything. It was midnight.

RIMMER: Oh, I seeee.

LISTER: Michelle. Michelle Fisher. God, she was gorgeous.

RIMMER: How old were you?

LISTER: Just gorgeous. If she'd have wanted, she could probably have got a job behind the perfume counter in Lewis's, that's how good looking she was.

RIMMER: How old were you?

LISTER: She took all her clothes off and just stood there in front of me, completely naked. I was so excited, I nearly dropped my skateboard.

RIMMER: Your *skateboard*? How old were you?

LISTER: Twelve.

RIMMER: Twelve!!! Twelve years old!!? You lost your virginity when you were twelve???

LISTER: Yeah.

RIMMER: Twelve?? (*Pause.*) Well, you can't have been a full member of the Golf Club, then.

LISTER: 'Course I wasn't.

RIMMER: You did it on a golf course, and you weren't a member?

LISTER: 'Course I wasn't.

RIMMER: You didn't pay any green fees or anything?

LISTER: It was just a place to go.

RIMMER: I used to play golf. I hate people who abuse the facilities. I hope you raked the sand back nicely before you left. That'd be a hell of a lie to get into, wouldn't it? Competition the next day, and your ball lands in Lister's buttock crevice. You'd need more than a niblick to get that one out.

LISTER: Are you trying to say I've got a big bum?

RIMMER: Big? It's like two badly parked Volkswagens. The

34

only things I ever lost when I was twelve were my shoes with the compass in the heel and the animal tracks on the soles. Porky Roebuck threw them in the septic tank behind the sports ground. I cried for weeks – I was wearing them. I never even thought about sex when I was twelve.

LISTER: Maybe that's because you used to be Alexander the Great's chief eunuch.

LISTER *starts tearing pages from a book and throwing them on to the fire.*

RIMMER: What are you doing?

LISTER: There's nothing left to burn.

RIMMER: But not my books! Don't burn the books.

LISTER: There's nothing else left.

RIMMER: But it's obscene. A book is a thing of beauty. The voice of freedom. It's the essence of civilization.

LISTER: (*Reads title*) Biggles' Big Adventure.

RIMMER: Well, perhaps not that one, but you know what I'm saying.

LISTER *throws it in the stove and picks up another one.*

LISTER: *Complete Works of Shakespeare.* That should be good for a couple of hours.

RIMMER: Three days without food, and the walls of civilization come tumbling down!

LISTER: What d'you mean?

RIMMER: They say that any society is only three meals away from revolution. Deprive a culture of food for three meals, and you'll have anarchy. And it's true, isn't it? You haven't eaten for a couple of days and you've turned into a barbarian.

LISTER: I'm just burning a book.

RIMMER: It's not just a book. It's the only copy of probably the greatest work in English literature. Probably the only copy left in the entire universe, and you're quite happy to toss it on the fire to keep your little mitts warm for fifteen minutes?

LISTER: There's nothing else to burn.

RIMMER: That's it, then, is it? Goodbye *Hamlet*? Farewell *Macbeth*? Toodle-pip *King Lear*?

LISTER: Have you ever read any of it?

RIMMER: I've seen *West Side Story*. That's based on one of them.

LISTER: Yeah, but have you ever actually read any?

RIMMER: Not all the way through, no. I can quote some, though.

LISTER: Go on, then.

RIMMER: (*Declaims grandly*) 'Now . . .' (*Long pause.*) That's all I can remember.

LISTER: Where's that from, then?

RIMMER: *Richard III*, you moron. That speech he does at the beginning. (*Declaims*) 'Now . . .' something something something. It's brilliant writing. It really is. Unforgettable.

LISTER: OK, I'll save it till last. (*Holds up another.*) *Lolita*. Is it OK if I burn *Lolita*?

RIMMER: Save page sixty-one.

LISTER *opens it and finds page sixty-one.* RIMMER *leans over his shoulder.*

RIMMER: That bit.

LISTER: That's disgusting.

He rips out page sixty-one, folds it into his pocket and throws the rest of the book on the fire.

14. Model shot
Starbug *in blizzard. Mix to:*

15. Int. Starbug rear. Day
Works of Shakespeare burning merrily on the fire. LISTER *is at the*

table. He picks up the dog food can, spoons out a generous lump of dog food in jelly, so it wobbles on his fork. RIMMER is watching him, appalled.

LISTER: And you can take that look off your face: like I'm doing something disgusting. I'm just trying to stay alive.

RIMMER: You're going to eat the dog food?

LISTER: I haven't eaten for six days. Yes, I'm going to eat the dog food.

RIMMER: I'm sure the dog food will be lovely.

LISTER: This isn't dog food. It's a piece of prime fillet steak in blue cheese sauce. It's been charcoal broiled in garlic butter. Mmmm. Just smell that. It's delicious. Delicious.

He pops the quivering mess into his mouth and swallows it.

LISTER: Well, now I know why dogs lick their testicles – it's to take away the taste of their food.

RIMMER: The stove's getting low. Better throw another book on.

LISTER: That's the last one.

RIMMER: What? You've burnt all of them?

LISTER: When we get through to Act Five of *Henry VIII*, I'm a dead man.

RIMMER: There must be something else to burn.

They both look around. At the same time, both of their eyes stop on the trunk.

RIMMER: No. It's Javanese camphor wood. It's priceless.

LISTER: There's nothing else left to burn except the trunk and what's in the trunk.

RIMMER: Now, wait a minute. Not Napoleon's Armée du Nord!

LISTER: Rimmer, get real, man. If it burns, we burn it. What's the least valuable?

RIMMER: Not the trunk. My father gave me that trunk.

LISTER: The soldiers, then.

RIMMER: They're nineteenth-century. They're irreplaceable. They were hand-carved by the legendary Dubois brothers.

LISTER: Well, then?

LISTER *brings out two huge wads of notes.* RIMMER *slightly glassy-eyed.*

16. Model shot
Starbug *in blizzard.*

17. Int. Starbug rear. Day
Shot: the stove. Money is burning. Another wad lands on top of it.

RIMMER: How much has gone so far?

LISTER: Five thousand eight hundred.

RIMMER: Five thousand eight hundred!

LISTER *throws on another wad.*

LISTER: Six grand.

RIMMER: The whole twenty-four grand isn't going to last an hour, is it? (*Nearly in tears*) It took me ten years to save that. Ten years!

LISTER: I'd better start unpacking the soldiers.

RIMMER: No. There must be something else to burn. There must be.

LISTER: There isn't. I've looked. Listen, I know it's a bummer. I know it must be heartbreaking. But it's only *stuff*. It's just possessions. In the end, they're not important. They might go for a bundle in some swanky Islington antique shop — but right here, and right now, all they are is nicely painted firewood.

LISTER *throws on some more money.*

RIMMER: This isn't happening. It's a nightmare.

LISTER: You've got to get your priorities right. It's like those people you read about who run back into a burning house to rescue some treasured piece of furniture and wind up burning to death. Nothing is more important than a human life . . .

RIMMER *is looking in the corner of the room.*

RIMMER: What about your guitar?

LISTER: . . . Except my guitar.

RIMMER: Why didn't we think of it before? We can burn your guitar.

LISTER: Not my *guitar*, Rimmer.

RIMMER: It's made of wood.

LISTER: Yeah, but it's my guitar. I've had it since I was sixteen. It's an authentic Les Paul copy.

RIMMER: But it's not worth anything. It's just a thing. It's just a possession.

LISTER: Yes, but it's mine.

RIMMER: How is it any different from my soldiers?

LISTER: It's my life-line. I . . . I need that guitar. When it gets to me – I mean the loneliness – when it gets on top of me . . . it's the only way I can escape. I mean, I know I'm not exactly a wizard on it, and it's only got five strings, and three of them are G, but the whole of my life I've never had anything to hang on to – no roots, no parents, no education . . .

RIMMER: No education?

LISTER: I went to art college. All I've ever had is that guitar. It's the only thing in the whole of my miserable smegging life that hasn't walked out on me. Don't make me burn it.

RIMMER: (*Quietly*) We've got to.

LISTER *hangs his head.*

LISTER: (*Pause.*) Look. This is going to sound pretty stupid . . . but I'd just like to play one more song on it. One for the road.

RIMMER: Sure, sure. I mean – I'm not enjoying this.
LISTER: I know. I, uh . . . Thanks, man.

LISTER *picks up the guitar, and walks off to a fairly dim corner. He strums a chord.* RIMMER *is looking at the floor, slightly embarrassed. In his most feeble, plaintive voice,* LISTER *begins to sing:*

LISTER: (*Singing*) 'She's Out Of My Life . . . She's Out Of My Life.' (*Spoken*) My step-dad taught me this one. First song I ever learned to play. (*Sings*) 'And I don't know whether to laugh or cry . . .'

RIMMER *gets up, embarrassed.*

RIMMER: I, uh, just, uh . . . (*Points at the door.*)

He walks up to the door.

18. Ext. Crashed Starbug. Blizzard
RIMMER *walks into the howling blizzard.*

19. Int. Starbug rear. Day
LISTER *puts down the guitar and nips over to the door to check Rimmer's gone. Carrying the guitar,* LISTER *nips over to the trunk, puts the guitar against the trunk, takes a pencil out of his top pocket and starts tracing the guitar shape on to the back of the trunk. He picks up a hacksaw.*

20. Ext. Crashed Starbug. Blizzard
RIMMER *looks at his watch, then back at the ship.*

21. Int. Starbug rear. Day
By now, LISTER *has removed a complete guitar shape out of the back of Rimmer's trunk. He pushes the trunk back against the wall,*

slips his guitar inside the green locker on the far wall, then crosses to the stove, and breaks the guitar-shaped piece of wood over his knee.

22. Ext. Crashed Starbug. Blizzard
RIMMER *walking up to the door.*

23. Int. Starbug rear. Day
The door opens and RIMMER *comes in.* LISTER *is sitting at the stove, guitar-shaped pieces of wood burning merrily away.*

RIMMER: I don't know what to say.

LISTER: Nothing *to* say.

RIMMER: You've made a supreme sacrifice. You know that? A *supreme* sacrifice.

LISTER: Had to be done.

RIMMER: I've been judging the book by its cover, haven't I? All these years, that's what I've been doing. But when it really comes down to it, you're one heck of a regular guy.

LISTER: (*Grunts*)

RIMMER: There's no point being modest. I know what that guitar meant to you. The same as that trunk means to me. If that trunk got so much as scratched, I'd be devastated. It's not the outward value – for me, that trunk is a link to the past. A link to the father I never managed to square things with . . .

LISTER: (*Slightly panicky*) Is it?

RIMMER: It's the only thing he ever gave me, apart from . . . apart from his disappointment.

LISTER *covers his face.*

RIMMER: But you've shown me, by burning your guitar, what true value is.

LISTER: (*Low moan.*)

RIMMER: Decency. Self-sacrifice. Those are the things that

make up real wealth. And from where I'm standing ...
I'm a pretty rich man.

LISTER: Oh, god.

RIMMER: Burn the soldiers.

LISTER: No. Not the soldiers too.

RIMMER: You burnt your guitar. I want to make a sacrifice,
too. Burn the Armée du Nord. Cast them to the flames: let
them lay down their lives for the sake of friendship. (*Sniffs
the air*) What's that smell?

LISTER: What smell? I can't smell any smell.

RIMMER: (*Sniffs*) Camphor.

LISTER: Oh, god.

RIMMER: Your guitar was made of camphor wood! It was
probably worth a fortune. Burn the soldiers – burn them
right now.

24. Ext. Blizzard

*We see two torches in the distance, coming towards us. Over, we
hear:*

KRYTEN: I can't go on.

CAT: You've got to go on, buddy: we're nearly there.

KRYTEN: I've no strength.

CAT: Come on, you can make it.

They come into view. KRYTEN *is pulling the heavily laden sleigh,
with the* CAT *sitting on it.* CAT *whips the air.*

CAT: Look – there they are. Mush! Mush!

25. Int. Starbug rear. Day

The soldiers are burning away. RIMMER *is peering into the stove.
After a while, he starts quietly imitating a trumpet, playing the 'last
post'. Finally, he finishes.*

RIMMER: *Au revoir, mes amis. A bientôt.*

LISTER: Look – there's something I've got to tell you . . . something awful.

RIMMER: If it's about how you finished off the dog food, Dave, I understand.

LISTER: No. It's not about that.

The door opens, and KRYTEN *and the* CAT *enter.*

CAT: Hey, hey, hey!

LISTER: Cat! Kryten! You made it – you found us!

RIMMER: So where've you been the last six days?

KRYTEN: We rendezvoused with Holly. Then, after two days, when you still hadn't turned up, I said we should go and look for you.

CAT: We have been everywhere. Fourteen moons, two planets. I've been so worried – I haven't buffed my shoes in two days.

RIMMER: So – Holly managed to navigate her way through five Black Holes?

HOLLY *appears on* KRYTEN's *chest monitor.*

HOLLY: As it transpired, there weren't any Black Holes.

RIMMER: But you saw them – you saw them on the monitor.

HOLLY: They weren't Black Holes.

RIMMER: What were they?

HOLLY: Grit. Five specks of grit on the scanner-scope. See, the thing about grit is, it's black, and the thing about scanner-scopes . . .

RIMMER: Oh, shut up.

LISTER: (*Sighs*) Come on. Let's go.

LISTER *and the* CAT *go out.*

RIMMER: Something happened here, Kryten. Something that made us closer. I saw a side of Dave Lister that I didn't even know existed. He's not just an irresponsible, selfish drifter, out for number one. He's a man . . . He's a Man of Honour.

LISTER *comes back in. Looking at the floor, he crosses to the locker.*

LISTER: Excuse me.

He opens the locker, takes out his guitar and exits. RIMMER *looks at the door, then at the fire, then, slowly, he turns to his trunk.*

RIMMER: Open the trunk.

KRYTEN *goes to open the trunk. We shoot through the guitar-shaped hole at the back of the trunk as the trunk opens, and* RIMMER *peers in. No expression. Without looking up:*

RIMMER: Kryten, would you get the hacksaw and follow me?
KRYTEN: Where are we going?
RIMMER: We are going to do to Lister what Alexander the Great once did to me.

DIMENSION JUMP

1. Model shot. Io
Caption: 'Io – third moon of Jupiter'. Mix to:

2. Model shot. Lunar landscape
There is a plastiglass dome which houses a city. Caption: 'Settlement population: 355,000'. Mix to:

3. Ext. Garden. Day
Caption: 'Rimmer household, 2162 AD'. Rimmer's mother is wandering down the garden, carrying a letter.

MRS RIMMER: (*Calls*) Arnold! Arnold!
YOUNG RIMMER: (*VO*) I'm here, Mother.

She looks in the direction of the voice. A SEVEN-YEAR-OLD *RIMMER is dangling from a tree. He's been tied, legs splayed, upside-down from a large branch. We see the word 'Bonehead' has been chalked on his back.*

MRS RIMMER: Arnold, you know your father and I have been terribly worried about your progress at school.
YOUNG RIMMER: Yes, mother.
MRS RIMMER: You just haven't been getting the marks we think you're capable of.
YOUNG RIMMER: No, mother.
MRS RIMMER: Well, a few days ago, I went in to see the

headmaster. He said it might be in your best interest if they kept you down a year. If you were to stay in Junior D for another year.

YOUNG RIMMER: Oh.

MRS RIMMER: Is that all you've got to say?

YOUNG RIMMER: Well, it's quite difficult to talk when you're tied upside-down to a tree.

MRS RIMMER: Have you been playing with Howard and Frank?

YOUNG RIMMER: Yes.

MRS RIMMER: What on earth were you playing?

YOUNG RIMMER: Well *I* said: 'It's such a shame we haven't got a swing,' and *they* said they could make one. I didn't realize they were going to make one out of me.

MRS RIMMER: That's nice, darling. Anyway. Your father had a word with the headmaster, and we explained how much we wanted you to be a test pilot in the Space Corps, like your brother John, and how this could damage your chances. We got this this morning. (*Starts opening the letter.*) You realize how important this is? This decision could completely alter the whole course of your life.

She reads the letter, giving nothing away, and looks at him.

4. Model shot. Space Corps landing pad

A gorgeous-looking space jet performs a vertical landing. Caption: 'Twenty years later: Space Corps Test Base, Miranda'.

5. Int. Test base corridor

Booted feet stride manfully along and step over the camera, accompanied by stirring music. A couple of boiler-suited technicians stand and applaud. And we reveal the boots belong to a devilishly handsome, blond-haired RIMMER: *Tom Cruise, James Bond and Flash Gordon all rolled into one. Humbly, he acknowledges their applause and rounds the corner, bumping into 'Spanners', who bears a striking resemblance to Lister.*

SPANNERS: Welcome home, Ace.

ACE RIMMER: Bless you, Spanners, old friend. (*They embrace manfully.*) It's good to be home.

SPANNERS: How did she behave?

ACE RIMMER: The light ship? Good as a frollicking filly in a harvest-time pasture. How you and your boys down in engineering got that crate to break the light barrier, I'll never know.

SPANNERS: Well, some people might say it's the devilishly brave and good-looking guy in the cockpit who did it.

ACE RIMMER: Tish, pshaw and nonsense. Any old twit can hug the event horizon of a Black Hole, then loop-de-loop round a spinning singularity at twice the speed of light, slam the engines into reverse and blast out of an imploding nebula. It's you and your guys with your magic wrenches, Spanners – you're the boys who break the records.

SPANNERS: I suppose you'll be going to this banquet thing they're throwing for you tonight.

ACE RIMMER: Good god, no. Heroes' welcomes with twenty-one-gun salutes in front of the entire Admiralty send me to the Land of Nod, Spanners. I'll be down in the mess with the salt-of-the-earth engineering boys as per usual. See you there at nineteen hundred?

ACE *slams* SPANNERS *playfully on the shoulder.*

SPANNERS: (*Sighs*) See you, Ace. (*Turns to the second technician.*) What a guy.

6. Int. Another part of corridor

ACE *strides up to a Space Corps* CHAPLAIN (*played by the Cat*).

CHAPLAIN: Welcome home, my son. You've been in all our prayers.

ACE RIMMER: Bless you, padré. How's little Tommy?

CHAPLAIN: He's pulled through. Be on his feet in no time, thanks to all that money you so generously . . .

ACE RIMMER: Now, padré. We agreed never to talk about that. It's a secret between you, me and (*Looks up Heavenward*) the Big Feller.

CHAPLAIN: But you saved that child's life.

ACE RIMMER: Tish, pshaw and nonsense, father. It's the surgeons. They're the chaps who deserve the praise.

CHAPLAIN: You're the one who kept that boy alive, my son: gave that little orphan child the will to live, sitting by his bedside day after day, night after night, holding his hand, reading him stories.

ACE RIMMER: You know me, Chaplain – any old excuse to get out of lunch with the Admiral. Nineteen hundred, we're having a bit of a bash in the mess. It would mean a lot to me if you were there.

ACE *goes off.*

CHAPLAIN: (*Sighs and shakes his head*) What a guy.

7. Int. Ante-room to Admiral's office. Day

MELLISSA, *the Admiral's adjutant* (*who looks like Holly*), *is behind a desk.* ACE *breezes in.*

ACE RIMMER: Commander Arnold Rimmer reporting for debriefing.

MELLISSA: So, you dog. You're back.

ACE RIMMER: Did you ever doubt it, when I've got someone like you to come back to?

MELLISSA: If only it were true. What are you doing for lunch?

ACE RIMMER: Not sure yet. Why?

MELLISSA: Because, if you're interested, I'll be in my quarters, covered in maple syrup.

ACE RIMMER: Sorry, Melly. You know I don't fraternize with the staff.

MELLISSA: I resign.

ACE RIMMER: I'll be there at thirteen hundred.

MELLISSA: Don't forget the maraschino cherries.

8. Int. Admiral's office. Day

Sign on desk reads: 'Admiral Sir James Tranter — Admiral of the Fleet'. The ADMIRAL *(played by a maskless* KRYTEN*) is signing papers.* ACE *comes in.*

TRANTER: You're back.

ACE: 'Fraid so.

TRANTER: I had a feeling you might be. Rubber shares went up this morning.

ACE: So, you wanted to see me, Bongo?

TRANTER: Ever heard of a thing called the Dimension Theory of Reality?

ACE: Doesn't it run along the lines that there is an infinite number of parallel universes, where every possibility exists?

TRANTER: It's along those lines. The basic tenet states that every decision that's made, the alternative decision is played out in another reality.

ACE: So?

TRANTER: So, the lab boys have come up with a drive that can break the speed of reality.

ACE: The boffins have hammered together a crate that can cross dimensions? When do I launch?

TRANTER: It's a one-way ticket, Ace. There's no coming back.

ACE *looks at his watch.*

ACE: I'm free at fifteen hundred.

TRANTER: You do understand — it's a prototype. There's no way of knowing if it'll even get there.

ACE: Where's 'there' exactly?

TRANTER: You'll be transported to an alternative reality: a reality where there's another Arnold Rimmer. Some decision was made at some point in your lives where he went one way and you went the other. You might well find he's quite different from you.

ACE: Sounds like quite a caper.

TRANTER: You'll do it?

ACE: I'm a test pilot in the Space Corps, Bongo. It's my job to do it.

TRANTER: I know it probably won't interest you, but I'd hate myself for the rest of my life if I didn't at least suggest it.

ACE: Suggest what?

TRANTER: If you're interested, I'll be in my quarters at lunchtime, covered in taramasalata.

ACE: Didn't know your bread was buttered that side, Bongo.

TRANTER: It isn't, Ace. Been happily married for thirty-five years. It's just – a chap like you can turn a guy's head.

ACE: Sorry, Bongo. Lunch is on Melly.

TRANTER: Would it make any difference if it was houmous?

ACE: Sorry, Bongo. I'm strictly butter-side-up.

TRANTER: Understood.

ACE *goes.*

TRANTER: What a guy.

9. Model shot. Landing pad

Ace's craft – a cross between a jet fighter and a dragster – stands ready for take-off.

10. Int. Ace's cockpit

ACE: All systems check. Let's get this kite up into the Big Black. Ignition. Chocks away.

Jets start up.

ACE: (*Shouts*) 'Bye, Bongo. 'Bye, Spanners. 'Bye, padré. 'Bye, Melly. Smoke me a kipper. (*Salutes.*) I'll be back for breakfast.

11. Int. Cargo bay area
SPANNERS, CHAPLAIN, MELLISSA *and* BONGO *all waving him off.*

ALL: 'Bye, Ace.
CHAPLAIN: God speed and bless you, son.

12. Model shot. Ace's jet takes off

13. Model shot. Red Dwarf in space

14. Int. Sleeping quarters. Night
Dark. LISTER *and* RIMMER *in bunks, asleep.* KRYTEN *appears in doorway, carrying a bag, a fishing rod and a fishing hat. He sets them down and creeps over to* LISTER. *He shakes* LISTER *to wake him, but gets no response. He looks nervously down to see if Rimmer's been disturbed. Shakes* LISTER *again.* LISTER *wakes up. He jumps down from the bunk, fully dressed, goes to the shower cubicle and brings out fishing gear and packed bag. They start to creep out of the sleeping quarters.* RIMMER *wakes.*

RIMMER: Lights!

Lights go up. LISTER *and* KRYTEN *freeze in mid-creep.*

RIMMER: What are you doing?
LISTER: (*Still frozen*) What?
RIMMER: What are you doing?
LISTER: What am I doing?

RIMMER: Yes. What are you doing?

LISTER: We're just nipping down the cinema – catch the midnight movie.

RIMMER: What? Dressed like that?

LISTER: Yeah. We're going to see *Jaws*.

RIMMER: You're going fishing, aren't you? That ocean planet we passed two days ago – you're going on a fishing holiday without me.

LISTER: Wha–at? Of course we're not, man. That's ridiculous.

CAT *creeps a few steps into the room, in full fishing gear – hat, rods, waders.*

CAT: (*Whispers*) *What are you doing with the lights on? Let's get out of here before . . .* (*Spots Rimmer and smiles, weakly.*)

RIMMER: I don't believe it. All three of you.

CAT: What's he talking about?

LISTER: I dunno – for some reason, he's got this whacked-out idea that all three of us were going on a fishing holiday.

CAT: A fishing holiday?

RIMMER *spots note pinned to fridge door. They all look at their feet.*

RIMMER: (*Reads*) 'Dear Rimmer, We have gone on a fishing holiday on the ocean planet we passed two days ago. We tried to wake you but couldn't. See you in three weeks. L., K. & C.'

KRYTEN: They made me do it, sir! I had no choice.

LISTER: (*Gritted teeth*) Kryten!

RIMMER: Why did you want to go without me?

LISTER: We didn't *want* to go without you. We just didn't think it was your scene. I mean, fishing – it's boring, isn't it?

RIMMER: I love fishing. The glow of the dawn – the line arcing into the water – netting the quarry and watching them slowly suffocate to death. Marvellous sport.

LISTER: That's it. That's exactly why we didn't invite you. There's no fish.

RIMMER: What?

KRYTEN: That at least is true, sir. We sent out a search probe, and there is no marine life on the entire planet.

LISTER: We just thought we'd sit out on Starbug, dangle the rods over the side, have a few cans, chill out.

RIMMER: I don't believe you. I don't believe anybody would go for a fishing holiday where they know there's no fish.

LISTER: We did it all the time back home. Used to go down the canal – there was never any fish in that. We went condom fishing. I swear, one time, I caught this two-pound black ribbed knobbler and it was (*Holds his hands eighteen inches apart*) this big.

RIMMER: Why didn't you just say: 'Rimmer, we're going on a fishing holiday, and we don't want you to come'?

CAT: See, man? That's what I said we should say!

RIMMER: I don't know what it is about me. All my life it's been the same story. It's not easy to look into that mirror every night and see a guy nobody likes.

CAT: How d'you think we feel? We have to look at it all day.

LISTER: Look, honestly – we just thought you wouldn't want to come.

RIMMER: I try to be liked. God knows, I try. I regale you with amusing stories of when I was treasurer of the amateur hammond organ owners' society ... you never laugh. I offer to talk you through my photo collection of twentieth-century telegraph poles, and you've always got some excuse. No one likes morris dancing. I mean, would that break your hearts, once in a while the four of us, getting our knees up in the air, the jingle of bells, the clonk of wood on wood? But, no, every time I suggest it, you all pretend to be ill.

LISTER: Look – you've got it wrong. We just thought you wouldn't want to come. Now we know you do, great –

come. The way you're going on about it, it's like we've been planning it for days, and there's some major conspiracy. There isn't.

RIMMER: Really?

LISTER: Really.

RIMMER: (*Thinks about it*) All right then. I'll just get changed. Holly?

HOLLY *appears on the screen, wearing a fishing hat with hooks in it.*

HOLLY: Oh, who woke him up?

15. Model shot. Starbug in space

16. Int. Starbug cockpit

KRYTEN *is driving,* RIMMER *sitting next to him.*

RIMMER: Steady, now, Kryten.

KRYTEN: Yes, sir.

RIMMER: Best to get there in one piece than to rush it and cause an accident.

KRYTEN: Sir, I have passed my test. I'm a fully qualified pilot.

RIMMER: Mind that star!

KRYTEN: (*Cranes forward*) Sir, that star is two light years away. We're nowhere near it.

RIMMER: There's no percentage in being a boy racer, Kryten. OK, you've passed your test, you're . . . Mind that planet!

KRYTEN: What planet?

RIMMER: That planet!

KRYTEN: That's the planet we're heading for, sir.

RIMMER: Excellent, excellent. Plot an orbital course. We'll be there in no time.

KRYTEN: I already have done, sir.

RIMMER: Yes, and get the second stage under way.

KRYTEN: I have done, sir.

RIMMER: But you haven't correlated the data with the main computer banks, have you?

KRYTEN: Yes, sir, I have, sir.

RIMMER: You know your trouble, Kryten? You're a git.

17. Int. Starbug rear

LISTER *seated, drinking lager.* CAT *next to him in a grump. They converse in stage whispers.*

CAT: (*Sotto*) I can't believe you were so stupid. Three weeks stuck with Captain Yawn!

LISTER: (*Sotto*) Look, it wasn't my fault – we could still have talked our way out of it if you hadn't blown the whole gaff.

CAT: (*Sotto*) Me? What did I do? You woke him up.

LISTER: (*Sotto*) I could have sweet-talked our way out of it but, oh no, you had to come blundering in with your size twelves . . .

CAT: (*Sotto*) You're so two-faced! Why haven't you got the guts just to tell the dude nobody likes him?

LISTER: (*Sotto*) Oh, yeah. Brilliant. What am I supposed to do? Go up to him and say, 'Excuse me, Rimmer, do you realize you're about as popular as a horny dog at a Miss Lovely Legs competition?'

CAT: (*Sotto*) Well, I would. That's what I'd do. I'd . . .

RIMMER *comes in from the cockpit section.*

CAT: (*Aloud, brightly*) Hi, buddy, how's it going?

RIMMER: Goh. I just had to get out of there. He's driving me nuts. I can't stand front-seat drivers. Come on, we're on holiday – let's cheer things up a bit. How about a little music? Where's my hammond CDs? Hands up for *Reggie Wilson Plays the Lift Music Classics*. No? OK, maybe something a bit more up-tempo – *Sounds of the Supermarket: Twenty Shopping Greats*.

CAT: Has anyone seen the key to the medicine cabinet? I feel a sudden urge to suffocate myself with a two-pound black ribbed knobbler.

LISTER: Not Reggie Wilson, Rimmer. Please.

RIMMER: You don't like Reggie Wilson? What? Not even *Pop Goes Delius* or *Funking up Wagner*?

LISTER: I'd prefer something a bit more melodious, like the drawn-out death rattle of a man suffering from terminal flatulence.

RIMMER: Come on, you bores. Let's do something. How about we sing some campfire songs? 'Kumbayah, my Lord, Kumbayah . . .' Come on, what's wrong with you? 'Kumbayah . . .'

HOLLY *appears on screen.*

HOLLY: Purple alert! Purple alert!

LISTER: What's a purple alert?

HOLLY: Well, it's sort of not as bad as a red alert, but a bit worse than a blue alert. More of a mauve alert . . .

RIMMER: Holly, wipe the rapid foam from your chin and start again.

HOLLY: Well, there's some sort of disruption to the time-fabric continuum. At least, I presume that's what it is. It's certainly got all the signs: it's a sort of large, wibbly, wavery, swirly thing, and it's coming straight towards us.

18. Int. Starbug cockpit

KRYTEN *is tapping at the keypad.* RIMMER *dashes in and leans over him.*

RIMMER: What is it?

KRYTEN: I don't know, sir. Whichever way I manoeuvre, it follows. It seems to be locked in on us. Wait – there's something coming out of it. Collision course! It's going to hit us.

KRYTEN *slams the panic button. SFX: alarm.*

19. Int. Starbug rear
We hear:

KRYTEN: (*VO*) Emergency, emergency: please adopt crash procedure.

RIMMER *dashes in.*

RIMMER: Where's the card? Who's got the card?
LISTER: What card?
RIMMER: The plastic card! The plastic card with the cartoons of the crash procedure on it!
LISTER: Rimmer, stop panicking.
RIMMER: It should be in the netting behind the seats! Haven't we all got to sit behind a woman clutching a baby? What's the drill?
LISTER: Look, I know what it is.
RIMMER: What?
LISTER: You sit down, tuck your head in your lap and brace yourself.

They all do.

RIMMER: Now what?

LISTER *passes* CAT *a magazine.*

LISTER: Then you open the in-flight magazine and start reading. The dullness of the articles acts as a sedative. I mean, just look at the contents list: 'Salt – an Epicure's Delight' ... 'Classic Wines of Estonia' ... 'Flemish weaving, the traditional way' ...
CAT: (*Sighs and starts looking drowsy.*)
LISTER: Don't fight it, man. Let it take you.
RIMMER: How can you be so mind-bogglingly flippant? Don't you realize what's going to happen? We're going to crash!

LISTER: You've got to stay calm. It's a known fact – the more relaxed you are, the less you're likely to be injured.

KRYTEN: (*VO*) Good luck, everybody – here it comes!

LISTER: (*Reads*) 'The salt on our table is something we far too often take for granted. But the history of salt is as old as civilization itself . . .'

20. Model shot

Ace's ship blasts into existence, strikes Starbug *a glancing blow, forcing it into a death dive.*

21. Int. Starbug rear

Camera tilted, so it looks like Starbug's *on a death dive. Over the scream of the engines, the three of them are reading out loud (but calmly).*

LISTER: (*Reading*) 'The Ancient Egyptians were great believers in salt, using it both in cooking and medication . . .'

Simultaneously, the CAT *is reading:*

CAT: (*Reading*) 'When most people think of classic wines, they are unlikely to consider the Estonian reds. Yet Estonian grapes are among the fruitiest and most subtle . . .'

And over them, RIMMER *is reading from the magazine at his feet:*

RIMMER: (*VO*) 'Since the beginning of the thirteenth century, Belgium has been the home of some of the most remarkable weaving ever to come out of north-west Europe . . .'

22. Model shot

Starbug *crashes into a sea, and smashes into a jutting rock. It's fairly dark, and the sea's quite stormy.*

23. Int. Starbug rear. Emergency lights

Debris all over the place. The three of them are lying half-conscious on the floor. There is an oil drum over the Cat's leg. KRYTEN *stumbles in from cockpit.*

KRYTEN: Is everyone all right?
RIMMER: Yes, thank god – I'm fine.
LISTER: Cat?
CAT: It's bad, buddy. It's real bad.

KRYTEN *and* LISTER *lift the drum off the Cat's leg. His trouser leg is torn and soaked with blood.*

CAT: See what I mean? Red with apricot. I look like a jerk. I'm bleeding an unfashionable colour! If I'd known my leg was going to get crushed, I'd have worn black – it goes with anything.
LISTER: Is anything broken?
CAT: Yeah – all the stitching's come away, and the lining's ripped. Someone help me – get me a tailor.
LISTER: Kryten, get the first-aid box. We'd better clean this up before he gets gangrene.
CAT: Gangrene? You think I might get gangrene? Hey – that might work. Green with apricot – I think I could carry that off.

KRYTEN *leans over him.*

KRYTEN: Looks like a break, sir. Quite a bad one. I'm going to have to snap the bone back into line. I'm afraid there's no anaesthetic.

The CAT *reaches for the in-flight magazine.*

CAT: (*Reads*) 'Salt – an Epicure's Delight. The salt on our table is something we far too often take for granted . . .'

KRYTEN *snaps his leg back into position with a sickening crack.*

CAT: (*Screams*) Oh, my god!

KRYTEN: Did it hurt?

CAT: What? No, I'm talking about the article. Have you done my leg yet?

RIMMER: What's the damage, Holly?

HOLLY: It doesn't look good. We've lost the starboard engine, the port engine's packed up, the fuel line's severed, we're taking in water through the hull, we've lost the landing jets, half the electrics are out and the elastic's snapped on the furry dice.

RIMMER: What does that mean in real terms?

HOLLY: Well, it means you've got a slightly more tasteful cockpit, but unless you fix that starboard engine, we'll start sinking in about forty minutes.

RIMMER: Anything we can do?

HOLLY: We could try and hire a dance band, and ask them to play 'Abide with Me'.

LISTER: I'm going to have to go out there and try and fix the engine.

RIMMER: You don't know anything about engines.

KRYTEN: Besides, there's a forty-knot gale out there, sir. It would be insane to even try. Only a fool or a hero would even consider it.

24. Int. Ace's cockpit. Night

Heroic music. ACE *is looking out of the side of the cockpit.*

ACE: Bingo! Down there – they've ditched into the drink. I'm baling out, computer.

COMPUTER: (*Sexy female voice*) But, Ace, it's a suicide mission.

ACE: I caused the smash. Should apologize – only manners. Bring her round for another pass.

COMPUTER: Please, Ace, don't go. I love you.

ACE: Stiff upper modem, old girl. Smoke me a kipper – I'll be back for breakfast.

25. Int. Starbug rear. Emergency lights

Airlock door spins open, and ACE *makes his entrance.*

ACE: The name's Commander Rimmer. Arnold Rimmer. Friends call me 'Ace'. Come from another dimension. Explain later. First, let's get you out of this pickle. (*To Kryten.*) And what do they call you, matey?

KRYTEN: Kryten, sir.

ACE: Series 4000 mechanoid. Am I right? Salt of the Space Corps. (*Slaps him on his shoulder and turns to Lister.*) Spanners!

LISTER: Eh?

ACE: Sorry – you reminded me of a fellow I once knew. What is your handle?

LISTER: Lister. Dave.

ACE: 'Course it is. Put it there, Dave. (*Shakes hands vigorously.*) You look like a great chap to be in a scrape with. And what about the guy in the sharp suit?

LISTER: He hasn't got a name – we just call him 'Cat'.

ACE: Looks like you bought a broken leg, Cat. Love your cuban heels. And who's the deeply delicious, stunningly gorgeous computer?

HOLLY: Holly. (*Swoons.*)

RIMMER *appears from the cockpit section.*

ACE: My god! It's me, only much more handsome. Well, looks like I'm superfluous here. Old Arnie'll have you out in no time.

LISTER: He's a hologram – he can't touch anything.

ACE: Golly. Dead, eh? Commiserations, old man – what a crushing bore that must be.

RIMMER: You're me?

ACE: Don't quite understand the science, but it's something to do with us living identical lives up until a certain point, where a decision was made and you went one way while I

61

went the other. Still, can't hang around chin-wagging. Let's get this box in the air. What's your plan, Arn?

RIMMER: I haven't got one.

ACE: (*Pause.*) Oh. (*Brightens.*) OK – this is what I suggest. The starboard engine looks repairable, but it's a two-man job. Any volunteers?

LISTER: Yeah, count me in. I've got a window in my schedule.

ACE: Not so fast, Davey boy. You leapt in so fast, you didn't give Arn a chance to speak. He was just about to volunteer, weren't you, Arn?

RIMMER: No, I wasn't.

ACE: Right. Well, let's get cracking. Arnie, what's the starboard engine's thrust-to-input ratio?

RIMMER: What's that?

ACE: Well, you can work it out: what's the craft's inertia rating?

RIMMER: (*Sheepish*) I don't know.

ACE: Well, what's the p.s.i.?

RIMMER: (*Irritable*) I don't know!

ACE: (*Pause.*) OK. We'll work it out when we get there. Come on, Dave. Best grab a brolly. There's a bit of a drizzle out there.

KRYTEN: Sir, may I have a word in private?

ACE: Of course, old friend. 'Scuse us.

26. Int. Starbug cockpit

KRYTEN *and* ACE *step in.*

ACE: What's the prob, Kryters?

KRYTEN: I have a limited knowledge of medicine, sir. But it's plainly obvious, even to me, that your left arm is broken in several places.

ACE: Took a bit of a tumble on the landing. Only a scratch.

KRYTEN: I can't allow you to go out in that storm, sir, with your arm in that condition. I must insist you allow me to go in your place.

ACE: I see. The series 4000 isn't waterproof, is it?

KRYTEN: That's beside the point, sir.

ACE: Look. Here's what we'll do . . .

Punches KRYTEN *and knocks him out, catches him and lowers him gently into a seat.*

ACE: Sorry, old chum. No option.

27. Int. Starbug rear. Emergency lights

ACE *steps back in.*

ACE: Arn, Kryten's taken a bit of a whack. Can you re-route his circuitry and bring him back on line?

RIMMER: How?

ACE: You don't know how to do that?

RIMMER: No.

ACE: Oh (*Little sigh.*) Come on, Dave. (*Slaps Lister on the shoulder.*) Let's catch a breath of fresh air. (*To Rimmer.*) Smoke me a kipper – can you do that? We'll be back for breakfast.

As ACE *turns his back,* RIMMER *gives him the finger.*

28. Ext. Starbug

LISTER *and* ACE *edge along the outside of* Starbug. *The storm roars.*

ACE: (*Shouts*) What's your favourite music, Dave?

LISTER: Eh?

ACE: Keeps your spirits up if you sing a song.

LISTER: I like Rastabilly skank.

They start singing as they edge along. Suddenly, LISTER *slips and dangles one-handed from a rail.* ACE *hangs on with his right arm and lowers his broken left arm for* LISTER *to catch hold of.*

ACE: Grab my arm, Davey.

LISTER *grabs Ace's broken arm. Close shot:* ACE *grimaces with bravely disguised agony. He hauls* LISTER *up to the ledge.*

ACE: Sorry, Dave. 'Fraid I'm going to have to do something a bit cissy now. Black out.

ACE *blacks out.* LISTER *keeps him upright. He comes to again.*

ACE: Sorry about that. Come on – let's get cracking.

They edge out of shot, singing.

29. Int. Starbug rear. Emergency lights

KRYTEN *is mopping the Cat's brow.*

CAT: (*Delirious*) Ohhhhh, paisley with stripes: nice match . . . Green anoraks with furry collars . . . they're great . . .

KRYTEN: Sir, he's delirious.

CAT: Ohhhhh . . . rubber over-trousers, held down with bicycle clips. Wow!

RIMMER *is pacing.*

RIMMER: 'Commander' Rimmer. I ask you. 'Ace'! Barf City. I bet you anything he wears women's underwear. They're all the same, his type. Rough and tumble, hurly-burly macho marines in public, and behind closed doors he'll be parading up and down in his taffeta ballgown, drinking mint julips and whipping the houseboy.

KRYTEN: Sir, he's you. It's just that your lives diverged at a certain point in time.

RIMMER: Yes – I went into the gents, and he went the other way.

KRYTEN: I assume, sir, you're making fatuous references to his sexuality. If I may point out . . .

Airlock door opens, and LISTER *and* ACE *burst in, in good spirits.*

64

LISTER: Yes! Yes! We did it.

LISTER *and* ACE *do the touch-up shuffle.*

ACE: What a team! How you got that housing clear, I will never know.

LISTER: Oh, come on, Ace – it was you. I could never have reconnected that fuel line.

ACE: Well, I couldn't have done it if you hadn't been holding me by the ankles.

LISTER: Yeah, but how you could hang upside-down and fix the starboard engine – it was just totally brutal.

ACE: What a team!

RIMMER: Wait! Now I know where I've seen you. Weren't you two the double-action centrefold in July's edition of *Big Boys in Boots*?

ACE: Now, look here, Arnold. You can say what you like about me, but I won't hear a word against Skipper here.

RIMMER: Skipper?

ACE: Chap like him needs a nickname. Thought Skipper sat rather well.

RIMMER: Ace and Skipper? You sound like a kids' TV series about a boy and his bush kangaroo.

ACE: Don't listen to him, Skipper. Let's get this tea chest up into the stars and back to the small rouge one.

RIMMER: Yes, the sooner we get back, the sooner you can climb into a nice soapy bath together and play 'Spot the Submarine'.

LISTER *holds* ACE *back.*

KRYTEN: Sir, the Cat. I don't think he's going to last much longer.

30. Model shot
Starbug *landing in Red Dwarf cargo bay.*

65

31. Int. Red Dwarf corridor

ACE, LISTER *and* KRYTEN *push the* CAT *along on a stretcher.* RIMMER *lags slouchily behind.*

CAT: (*Moaning*) Ohhhh . . . Bri-nylon underwear . . . sock suspenders . . . suits with cardigans . . . Ohhhh . . .

KRYTEN: He's getting worse, sir. His leg's all swollen. I think . . . I think he may lose it.

LISTER: Lose his leg?

KRYTEN: I fear so. The operation required to save it is beyond my expertise.

CAT: (*Weakly*) Lose my leg? Oh that's terrible – none of my suits will fit. (*Faints.*)

ACE: Kryten, I'll need 500 c.c.s of cortico-adrenaline, two pints of plasma, a laser scalpel and some kind of tissue sampler – the Macro-Bollington will do.

RIMMER: Oh, my god . . .

ACE: Field micro-surgery – all part of basic training in the Space Corps Special Service. I'll go and scrub up.

RIMMER: I'll go and *throw* up.

32. Int. Sleeping quarters. Day

RIMMER *is sitting, with his legs up on the table.* LISTER *enters.*

RIMMER: How's the Cat?

LISTER: Ace did it. Cat's fine, now. He's just sitting up in bed looking through some swatches, trying to pick a material he likes for his dressings. I don't know how Ace does it. He's been on his feet for thirty-six hours now. He's still laughing and joking. What a guy! He's just nipped off to teach Kryten how to play the piano. Amazing dude.

RIMMER: So: is it going to be a simple Register Office or a full church do for you two?

LISTER: I don't understand your attitude, Rimmer. He's you.

RIMMER: No, he's not me. I'm me. He's a me who had all the breaks, all the luck, all the chances I never got.

LISTER: No. It was just a single incident, and your lives went off in completely different directions. It's incredible that just one decision in your childhood could produce such drastically different people.

RIMMER: Right. He probably got to go to some really great school, while I was lumbered with Io House. He got to meet all the right people, greased his way up the old-boy network, towel-flicked his way into the Space Corps, Masonic handshook his way into Flight School and brown-tongued his way up the ranks.

LISTER: You think you'd be pleased that somewhere in some dimension there's another you who's doing really well for himself.

RIMMER: How would you feel if some git arrived from another dimension – another Lister with wall-to-wall charisma and a Ph.D in being deeply handsome and wonderful?

LISTER: Hey, man – I *am* that Lister.

RIMMER: No, come on. How would you feel if there was another Lister doing a hell of a lot better than you?

LISTER: There is. Ace knows him. That's why he called me 'Spanners' when he first came in. In Ace's dimension, he's a Flight Engineer for the Space Corps. Married to Kristine Kochanski. Twin sons – Jim and Bexley. I've made up for him. Whatever he did that I didn't, he deserves the lot. For me, it kind of makes sense of a lot of stuff to know that, in all these dimensions, every possibility's played out. Hell, there's probably some weird dimension out there where you're better-looking than me.

RIMMER: Well, it just makes me bitter. You know, I've always had this thing about not getting the breaks. And there's living proof of what I could have achieved if I'd got the one he got.

Off, we hear a knock and:

ACE: (*VO*) Skipper? Got a mo?

LISTER *gets up*.

RIMMER: Go on – he's probably picked out a ring.

33. Int. Outside sleeping quarters

ACE *is standing in the corridor, sewing up the wound on his arm.*
LISTER *comes out.*

ACE: I've decided I'm not going to stay, Skipper.
LISTER: Why?
ACE: Him and me – it would never work. I just can't stand to
be near him: to see myself so bitter, so warped and weasly.
The man's a maggot.
LISTER: So where are you going to go?
ACE: Can't go back, but there are a billion other realities to
explore – a billion other Arnold Rimmers to meet. Maybe
somewhere there's one who's more of a pain in the butt
than him, but I doubt it.
LISTER: Good luck, man. And don't be too hard on Rimmer.
You got the break – he didn't. He's just bitter.
ACE: You know what the break was? At the age of seven,
one of us was kept back a year; the other wasn't. (*Finishes
sewing – offers his arm.*) Put your finger on that, will you,
Skipper?

LISTER *puts his finger on the stitches.* ACE *bites the cat gut and
flexes his hand.*

LISTER: And that was the only difference? Rimmer was held
down a year, and you went up?
ACE: No. I was the one held down. By his terms, he got the
lucky break. But being held down made me. The humilia-
tion. Being the tallest boy in the class by a clear foot. It
changed me; made me buckle down, made me fight back.
And I've been fighting back ever since.

LISTER: While he's spent the rest of his life making excuses.

ACE: Maybe he's right. Maybe I did get the lucky break. Well, I'll grab my things and be off. Smoke me a kipper, Skipper. (*Salutes.*) I'll be back for breakfast.

ACE *goes.* LISTER *watches him.*

34. Int. Corridor. Day

ACE *striding along, very much like the opening.*

A recess. RIMMER *is on his haunches with a* SKUTTER, *who has a rope in his mouth. We follow the rope, which goes up to the ceiling, where it is attached to a net full of kippers.*

RIMMER: Ready?

SKUTTER *nods.*

RIMMER: I'll smoke him a smegging kipper.

Back to: ACE *striding towards the net. Back to:* RIMMER *and* SKUTTER.

RIMMER: (*Mouths*) Now!

SKUTTER *tugs the rope. Back to:* ACE *strides under the net. Nothing happens. He shakes his head and carries on.*

35. Model shot

Accompanied by heroic music, Ace's ship leaves Red Dwarf. Over, we scroll the caption: 'In the decades that followed, Ace Rimmer searched countless realities and met thousands of Arnold Rimmers. However, he never encountered an Arnold Rimmer as deeply sad and worthless as the one he had met aboard Red Dwarf. His impossible search continues . . .' *And Ace's ship blasts off for another dimension.*

36. Model shot. Red Dwarf in space

Over, we hear:

RIMMER: (*VO*) It's Wednesday night – it's amateur hammond organ night. OK, take it away, skutters.

JUSTICE

1. Int. Medical unit. Morning

LISTER *is in the medical bed. His head has swollen to the size and shape of the Mekon's.* KRYTEN *wheels in a breakfast trolley.*

KRYTEN: How are you feeling, sir?

LISTER: (*Weakly*) Ohhh, much better, thanks, man.

KRYTEN: You certainly look better. I can't believe how much the swelling's gone down overnight.

LISTER: You reckon?

KRYTEN: Definitely. It was almost interfering with the ceiling fan yesterday afternoon. You're nearly back to your old self. In fact, you can hardly tell you've got space mumps at all.

LISTER: Can I have a mirror?

KRYTEN *takes out enormous head-measuring device.*

KRYTEN: I don't think you're quite ready for a mirror yet, sir. Let's take it one step at a time.

Measures Lister's head.

KRYTEN: What did I tell you? It's gone down eight inches overnight. You'll be up and about in no time.

LISTER: I don't know what I'd have done without you this last three weeks. Florence Nightingdroid. Did you bring me breakfast?

KRYTEN: Yes, sir. Hot lager with croutons, just the way you asked.

LISTER *lifts the lid of the soup bowl and starts to spoon up the lager.*

LISTER: Well, you certainly find out who your mates are when you've got an unsightly, disfiguring ailment.

KRYTEN: Oh, I wouldn't say 'unsightly', sir.

LISTER: Oh, come on, Kryten. I've got a head like a hot-air balloon. I look like the Human Lightbulb. And how many times have they dropped in with a word of comfort or a bunch of grapes?

KRYTEN: It's just not been possible, sir. Mr Rimmer has been on vacation.

LISTER: The world's most charismatic man? Where did he go?

KRYTEN: On a rambling holiday through the diesel decks. A ten-day hike through the ship's combustion engines with two of the skutters. He said he'd pop in later and show you the slides.

LISTER: (*Worried*) He didn't, did he?

KRYTEN: He's been loading the projection carousel for twenty-four hours now.

LISTER: You've got to stop him. A slide show of the diesel decks – that could finish me. (*Sighs.*) I'd have thought the Cat might have dropped in, though.

KRYTEN: Well, he's been a little preoccupied of late with this pod business. (*Curses himself.*) Oh, screw down my diodes and call me Frank! I wasn't supposed to mention that.

LISTER: What pod?

KRYTEN: Sir, you're not well – just forget I mentioned it.

LISTER: Come on, what pod?

KRYTEN: Yesterday evening we came across an escape pod floating in the local asteroid belt. It contains the survivor of some space crash, apparently cryogenically frozen.

LISTER: Oh, yeah?

KRYTEN: All the signs are she's in suitable condition for re-vival.

LISTER: She?

KRYTEN: As far as we can tell, she's a she.

LISTER: Oh, that's great, isn't it? That's just typical. The first female company in three million years, and I look like something that belongs up a whale's nose.

LISTER *gets up.*

KRYTEN: You can't get up, sir. What are you doing?

LISTER: There's a woman on board – what d'you think I'm doing? I'm on the cop.

2. Int. Sleeping quarters. Morning

Space-worn escape pod, just large enough for a person. LISTER *is examining the pod.*

LISTER: (*Reading*) 'Barbra Bellini'. What a beautiful name. There's no justice. How could this happen to me?

CAT *comes in.*

LISTER: Maybe I could wear a turban and pretend I'm from India.

CAT: Maybe you could stick a spike in your head and pretend you're the Taj Mahal.

LISTER: Oh, it's you. Well, thanks for visiting me. Thanks a lot.

CAT: You know what you look like? You could go out double-dating with the Elephant Man, and he would be the looker.

LISTER: (*Examining pod*) Why isn't it activated? How come no one's started the thaw process?

CAT: What? I thought Alphabet Head did it.

CAT *presses a few buttons on the keypad, and lights begin to glow. On the pod the display reads '29 hrs 59 mins 57 secs to revival' and the seconds count down.*

LISTER: So who is she? Where did she come from?

CAT: (*Caressing pod*) Who cares? At last – a date.

LISTER: Who says she's going to be interested in you?

CAT: I see what you're saying. All that time alone in Deep Space could have driven her insane.

LISTER: No. Say she's just an ordinary woman   ho doesn't go for your type.

CAT: No – I'd have heard about her. She'd have appeared in Ripley's *Believe It or Not*.

LISTER: Say she prefers someone else?

CAT: Like who?

LISTER: I dunno. Like me?

CAT: (*Smiles*) Buddy, you've got a head like a watermelon. What are you going to do? Paint it with orange and black stripes and tell her you play quarterback with the Bengals?

LISTER: I just think you're a bit cocky for a guy who's never actually met a real woman before.

CAT: I've seen mirrors. I have eyes. Face it, buddy – I have a body that makes *men* wet. You ever heard of an animal called the Iranian jerd? It can do 150 pelvic thrusts a second.

LISTER: So?

CAT: That's me in slo-mo. Put a Black and Decker drill on the end, I can make it through walls.

RIMMER *enters with* KRYTEN.

RIMMER: Listy, what are you doing up? Shouldn't you be in the greenhouse with the rest of the cantaloupes? (*Notices pod.*) Who started the R.P.?!

CAT: What's the problem? She's in there, let's get her out.

RIMMER: The problem, pussycat Willum, is this capsule was ejected from a prison ship, on which the convicts mutinied. There was a pitched battle, with only two survivors: one prisoner and one guard – the erstwhile Ms Bellini. One of those two got into this pod and escaped. But, of course, you'll know all this, having familiarized yourself thoroughly with the black-box recording.

LISTER: So, if it's not Bellini in there, who is it?

RIMMER: One of the prisoners. And considering the ship was transporting forty psychotic, half-crazed, mass-murdering, super-strong androids, we thought it prudent to find out who the smeg was in there before we woke them up.

KRYTEN: With respect, sir, they're not androids. They're simulants.

CAT: What's the difference?

KRYTEN: Well, the basic difference is that an android would never rip off a human's head and spit down his neck.

LISTER: Can we stop it, Hol?

HOLLY: No. One-way process.

LISTER: Can't we find out who's inside by x-raying the pod?

HOLLY: No. Lead lining. Has to survive in space.

LISTER: There must be some way.

HOLLY: Oh, there is: all you have to do is hang around here for twenty-four hours. Then, if you suddenly turn round and find your limbs are scattered around Deep Space and your necks are full of saliva, you can take it as read it probably wasn't Babs.

CAT: Why not tool up with bazookoids, wait for the pod to open, and if it's one of these bad-ass android dudes, let it eat laser?

KRYTEN: Simulants are almost indestructible, sir. It could easily withstand a volley of bazookoid fire at close range. It would certainly survive long enough to make balloon animals out of your lower intestines.

RIMMER: Well, I see no other option. Let's blast it back into space.

LISTER: Say it isn't a simulant? We can't just shoot an innocent woman into space.

CAT: What a dilemma! Inside that pod is either death or a date. Personally, I'm prepared to take the risk.

RIMMER: Meanwhile the pod is defrosting, and we still haven't decided what to do. Any ideas, Holly?

HOLLY: Here's a possibility: the black box contains the co-ordinates of the penal colony the prison ship was heading for. There are bound to be facilities there to contain any hostile form. If it turns out to be Bellini, we release her. If it's the simulant, we can bung him in a cell and leave him to rot.

RIMMER: If the colony's still there, and if it's operational.

KRYTEN: There's an old android saying, which, I believe, has particular relevance here. Goes like this: 'If you don't gosub a program loop, you'll never get a subroutine.'

LISTER: We have a human saying that means the same thing: nothing ventured, nothing gained.

KRYTEN: I think the android one is punchier.

3. Model shot. Starbug in space

4. Int. Starbug cockpit section

The CAT *is piloting.* LISTER *is beside him, still with his swollen head.*

CAT: You have to sit up here?

LISTER: It's warmer in the front. Seems to help my gunge.

CAT: I can't see anything. Your head keeps getting in the way of the mirror. In fact, your head keeps getting in the way of the windscreen.

From the rear section we hear:

RIMMER: (*VO*) Next! Ah, now, this one . . .

5. Int. Starbug rear section

Black screen. Shot of RIMMER *in hiking gear, standing next to an incredibly boring piece of machinery with a* SKUTTER, *slides into view.*

RIMMER: We reached this beauty on the evening of the fourth day. The Cameron–Mackintosh forty-valve, air-cooled diesel – the 184 – it's almost identical to the 179, but have you noticed the difference? Can you see the refinement in the funnel edgings?

Reaction: KRYTEN *watching, obviously in pain.*

RIMMER: I thought: we're not going to get another chance to see one of these, so we bivouacked down under the fuel pump for the night. There's a funny story about that, which I'll tell you later. But we're not going to get to any of the class fives unless we push along. Next!

Another slide.

KRYTEN: Sir, can we just take a break for a while? My intelligence circuits appear to have melted.

RIMMER: Well, we're not going to get through them all if we have a second break.

KRYTEN: Sir, that's a gamble I'm willing to take.

From the front section, we hear a sort of soggy explosion. There is a pause.

CAT: (*Revolted*) Oh, my goddddd!

LISTER: Ah! That's better.

CAT *staggers in, covered in yellow slime.*

CAT: His . . . head . . . burst!

LISTER *wanders in behind him. His hair is all matted, and skin is dangling from his head. He tears a bit off and grins amiably.*

LISTER: Oh, man, that is so much better. I feel great. Talk about a weight off your mind.

CAT: I don't want to live. Someone, please. Shoot me in the head.

6. Model shot
Penal colony space station. Starbug *approaching.*

7. Int. Starbug cockpit
Everyone is crowding around LISTER, *seated in drive seat.*

LISTER: Anything down there, Hol?

HOLLY: No life forms, not according to the heat scan.

KRYTEN: Any mechanical intelligence?

HOLLY: Yeah. The mainframe's still operational. Just initiating interface. Hang about. Here we go. Getting a message.

Holly's voice changes to deep, husky male.

JUSTICE COMPUTER: Welcome to Justice World. Please state your clearance code and prison officer ident.

LISTER: We're not a prison ship. We don't have a clearance code. We just want to use your facilities.

JUSTICE COMPUTER: State life-form inventory.

RIMMER: Four: one hologram, one mechanoid, two humanoid.

JUSTICE COMPUTER: Transfer ship navicomp to my jurisdiction.

LISTER *flips a switch.*

JUSTICE COMPUTER: On landing, please disembark and proceed through the neutral area to the clearance zone.

8. Model shot
Starbug *swoops towards the colony.*

9. Int. Corridor on colony
CAT, KRYTEN, RIMMER *and* LISTER *walk along derelict corridor. Sign on the wall reads 'Neutral Area'.*

JUSTICE COMPUTER: (*Over*) Until you are granted a clearance code, please observe all security requirements. Your party will be met by a consignment of escort boots.

They exchange glances. From around the corner, four pairs of disembodied boots walk down the corridor towards them. The boots look like metal versions of concrete boots. Electronic lights decorate them. The boots walk up to them, split open.

JUSTICE COMPUTER: Please step into the boots.

LISTER *stands inside one pair of the boots, and they close around his feet.* CAT *steps into his boots.*

CAT: I'm supposed to wear these? They look like Franken-stein's hand-me-downs. You haven't got anything with a cuban heel or a crêpe sole?

RIMMER: I can't use these – I'm a hologram.

JUSTICE COMPUTER: That has been accounted for.

RIMMER *and* KRYTEN *step into their boots.*

LISTER: Now what?

The boots light up, and all four of them lurch forward as the boots escort them down the corridor, in a variety of funny walks.

10. Int. Another corridor on Justice World
They file down the corridor. Each of them pauses under a cone of blue light.

LISTER: What's this?

KRYTEN: Relax, sir. It's just a mind-probe.

And the boots lead them on.

11. Int. Clearance zone
The boots escort them to the middle of the room.

LISTER: What's a mind-probe?

KRYTEN: The computer was merely searching our minds – presumably for evidence of criminal activity.

LISTER: Whu-what d'you mean, criminal activity?

KRYTEN: I shouldn't worry, sir. It's just a routine clearance procedure.

LISTER: So when you say 'criminal activity', whu-whu-what exactly d'you mean by 'criminal activity'? How criminal do you mean by criminal?

RIMMER: What are you bleating on about, Lister?

LISTER: Just define 'criminal activity' for me.

KRYTEN: Well, imagine a situation where someone had committed a crime and concealed it from the law, the mind-probe would be able to uncover that crime and sentence that person accordingly.

LISTER: Why did nobody tell me about this before we put the smegging boots on?

RIMMER: Oh, Listy, Listy. Is that a small sewage plant you're carrying in your trousers, or do I detect you're a tad concerned?

LISTER: Well, come on, guys – everyone has done something in their past that's a little bit illegal.

RIMMER: I haven't. I've never so much as got a parking fine.

LISTER: Yeah, but most people . . . I mean, everyone I knew . . . Aw, smeggin' hell.

CAT: So what did you do?

LISTER: Well, I mean, like scrumping. I mean, when I was a kid, back in Liverpool, we all used to go scrumping.

KRYTEN: Stealing apples? That's hardly a crime.

LISTER: Yeah, but me and my mates – we went scrumping for cars.

RIMMER: Did you get caught?

LISTER: All the time. I was stupid.

KRYTEN: Well, that's no problem then. You've served your punishment.

LISTER: Yeah, but there was other stuff as a kid. Stuff I didn't get caught for.

RIMMER: Like what?

LISTER: There was one time at this hotel . . .

KRYTEN: Oh, lots of people take towels from hotels.

LISTER: I took the bed. Winched it out of the window to my mate outside. I was renting this flat. It was unfurnished.

RIMMER: So you went to a hotel and stole the bed?

LISTER: I stole the entire room, actually. Armchair, dressing-table, carpet. Even the fitted wardrobe. The only thing I didn't take were the towels. I'm not proud of it.

RIMMER: Absolutely despicable. You are a common thief.

LISTER: I'm not making excuses, but everyone was doing it. I wasn't strong enough to go against the flow.

CAT: Well, I wouldn't like to be in your boots right now, buddy.

LISTER: What's going to happen to me?

KRYTEN: I wouldn't worry about it, sir. I'm sure they're not interested in a minor misdemeanour you committed as an adolescent over three million years ago.

LISTER: Seriously, Kryten: you reckon?

KRYTEN: (*Brightens*) Boy, I'm really getting the hang of this 'lie mode'. That was totally convincing, wasn't it?

JUSTICE COMPUTER: The mechanoid Kryten: clearance granted. You may go freely about the complex.

Kryten's boots release him. He steps free.

JUSTICE COMPUTER: The creature known as Cat: clearance granted.

The Cat's boots release him.

JUSTICE COMPUTER: The human known as Lister: despite a number of petty criminal acts: clearance granted.

LISTER *closes his eyes. We hear boots release him.*

JUSTICE COMPUTER: The hologram known as Rimmer. Guilty of second-degree murder. One thousand, one hundred and sixty-seven counts.

RIMMER: No . . . There's some mistake, surely . . .

JUSTICE COMPUTER: Each count carries a statutory penalty of eight years' penal servitude. In the light of your hologramatic status, these sentences are to be served consecutively, making a total sentence of nine thousand, three hundred and twenty-eight years.

RIMMER: I've never so much as returned a library book late. Second-degree murder? A thousand people? I would have remembered.

JUSTICE COMPUTER: Your wilful negligence in failing to re-seal a drive plate resulted in the deaths of the entire crew of the Jupiter Mining Corporation vessel the Red Dwarf.

RIMMER: (*Pause.*) Oh, that.

JUSTICE COMPUTER: Sentence to commence immediately.

Rimmer's boots light up, and he is frogmarched out of the room.

12. Int. Another corridor on the colony

RIMMER *is being marched along in his escort boots. He passes under a strange archway bathed in a strange light.*

JUSTICE COMPUTER: You are now leaving the Neutral Area and entering the Justice Zone. Beyond this point, it is impossible to commit any act of injustice.

RIMMER: (*Quietly*) Help.

13. Model shot. Justice World

14. Int. Rimmer's apartment. Day

A white room – fairly spartan, but it certainly doesn't look like a prison cell. Bed, table, etc. RIMMER *is sitting forlornly on the bed in some futuristic prison garb.* LISTER *comes in.*

LISTER: Hi, Killer.

RIMMER: Nine thousand years. Nine!

LISTER: I brought you a book.

LISTER *tosses book on bed.*

RIMMER: Oh, thanks. That'll help the centuries fly past.

LISTER: Look, don't panic, man. We're going to get you out of here.

RIMMER: Why bother? I'll be up for parole in a couple of Ice Ages.

LISTER: Kryten reckons you've got right of appeal. He's trying to get a case together. (*Looks round.*) This isn't a bad place for a prison. How come there are no locks or bars or guards or anything?

RIMMER: There doesn't need to be. The whole prison complex is covered by something called a Justice Field. I had to sit through this lecture. Apparently it's physically impossible to commit any kind of crime here.

LISTER: What d'you mean?

RIMMER: Try and commit a crime. You'll see.

LISTER: Like what?

RIMMER: I don't know. Anything . . . Arson. Try and set fire to those blankets.

LISTER: Eh?

RIMMER: Just try it.

LISTER *crosses to the blankets, takes out his Zippo and holds the flame under the blanket. The blanket doesn't ignite, but Lister's jacket starts smoking at the back.* LISTER *doesn't realize.*

RIMMER: Whatever crime you try and commit, the consequences happen to you.

LISTER: I'm not with you.

Feels the heat from the back of his flaming jacket.

LISTER: Smegging hell!

Takes his jacket off and jumps up and down on it.

LISTER: Nice example, Rimmer! You couldn't just have explained that to me verbally?

RIMMER: Same with stealing. Same with everything.

LISTER: *With* you. So if you nick something, something of yours goes missing?

RIMMER: Right. Try it.

LISTER: (*Pause while he thinks about it.*) No.

RIMMER: See? It's the perfect system. It forces the inmates to adhere to the law. And when they get out, it's become second nature.

KRYTEN *enters, followed by the* CAT.

KRYTEN: Good news. The Justice Computer has sanctioned a re-trial. I think we have a very strong case.

RIMMER: You do?

KRYTEN: It's a question of differentiating between guilt and culpability, sir. What the mind-probe detected was your own sense of guilt about the accident. In a way, you tried and convicted yourself. I simply have to establish you're a neurotic, under-achieving emotional retard whose ambition far outstrips his minuscule abilities and who consequently blames himself for an accident for which he could not possibly have been responsible.

RIMMER: You're going to prove that I was innocent of negligence on the grounds that I'm a half-witted incompetent?

CAT: Man, there ain't a jury in the land that won't buy a plea like that.

KRYTEN: Not a half-wit, exactly – more a buffoon.

RIMMER: (*Thinks about it. He's quite impressed.*) Right, I see. But how would you even begin to build such a case? Where would you conjure up the evidence?

KRYTEN: Sir, providing I can have completely free access to

your personal data files, I think I could come up with the outline of a winning case by lunchtime.

15. Model shot
Starbug *at rest in Justice World landing bay. Mix to:*

16. Int. Clearance zone. Day
LISTER *and the* CAT *look on.* RIMMER *is seated in his dress uniform with long-service medals.* KRYTEN *addresses the court.*

KRYTEN: The mind-probe was created to detect guilt, yet in the case of Arnold Judas Rimmer the guilt it detected attaches to no crime. He held a position of little or no authority on Red Dwarf. He was a lowly grease-monkey, a nothing, a piece of sputum floating in the toilet bowl of life.

Shot: RIMMER, *unsure how to react.*

KRYTEN: Yet he could never come to terms with a lifetime of under-achievement. His absurdly inflated ego would never permit it. He's like the security guard on the front gate who considers himself head of the corporation. So, when the crew were wiped out by a nuclear accident, Arnold Rimmer accepted the blame: it was his ship, ergo his fault. I ask the court: look at this man. This man who sat and failed his astronavigation exam on no less than thirteen occasions. This sad man, this pathetic man, this joke of a man, this . . .

RIMMER: (*Discreetly*) Kryten. You're going over the top. The computer will never buy it.

KRYTEN: Trust me, sir. My whole case hinges on proving you're a dork.

RIMMER: (*Reluctantly*) Understood.

KRYTEN: (*Aloud*) I call my first witness.

LISTER *crosses to stand, wearing some sort of apology for a tie.*

KRYTEN: Name?

LISTER: Dave Lister.

KRYTEN: Occupation?

LISTER: (*Thinks about it. Shrugs.*) Bum.

KRYTEN: Would you describe the accused as a friend?

CAT: (*Calls*) Take the Fifth!

KRYTEN: Answer the question, please. Remember, you're under polygraphic surveillance. Would you describe the accused as a friend?

LISTER: No, I would describe the accused as a git.

KRYTEN: Who would you say, then, is the person who thinks of him most fondly?

LISTER: (*Thinks about it, and answers truthfully*) Me.

KRYTEN: And there are no others who've shared moments of intimacy with him?

LISTER: Only one. But she's got a puncture.

RIMMER: Objection.

JUSTICE COMPUTER: Overruled.

KRYTEN: So you wouldn't describe him as a man with a good social life?

LISTER: He partied less than Rudolf Hess. He was totally dedicated to his career. He was in charge of Z shift, and it occupied his every waking moment.

KRYTEN: And what was Z shift's most important duty?

LISTER: Well, we had lots of duties around the ship, but I suppose our most vital responsibility was making sure the vending machines didn't run out of fun-size Munchie Bars.

KRYTEN: Can you envisage a situation where the lack of honeycomb-centred chocolate bars might be the direct cause of a lethal radiation leak?

LISTER: Not off the top of my head, no.

KRYTEN: (*Turns*) I ask the court one key question: would the Space Corps have allowed this man (*Points at Rimmer*)

Craig Charles (Lister)
before and after 50 m.p.h.
snowstorm composed of
laxative flakes ('Marooned')
(Photographer: Paul Grant)

Polymorph – Red Dwarf's
first animatronic guest
('Polymorph')
(Photographer: Paul Grant)

Kryten (Robert Llewellyn) in
cold-ear mode ('Marooned')
(Photographer: Paul Grant)

These boots are made for escorting ('Justice')
(Photographer: Mike Vaughan)

Starbug mid-section, built purely for 'Marooned',
destined to replace Red Dwarf by Season Six

Home sweet home – the sleeping quarters

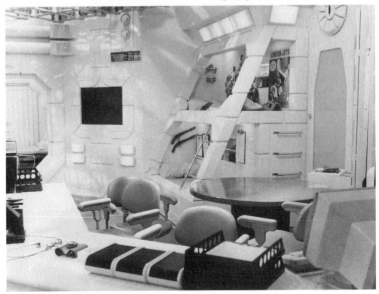

Clockwise from bottom left:
Scaffolding holding up the audience
seating doubles as a crashed spaceship in
'Camille' (Photographer: Mike Vaughan)
Lister (Craig Charles) lines up his
bazookoid (Photographer: Mike Vaughan)
Smoke him a kipper – he'll be back for
breakfast (Chris Barrie as Ace Rimmer)
(Photographer: Mike Vaughan)

Holly (Hattie Hayridge)
(Photographer: Mike Vaughan)

Cat (Danny John-Jules)
(Photographer: Mike Vaughan)

Rimmer (Chris Barrie)
(Photographer: Mike Vaughan)

Lister (Craig Charles)
(Photographer: Mike Vaughan)

Tim Spall – what a twonk ('Back to Reality')
(Photographer: Mike Vaughan)

'I have teeth the Druids could use as a place of worship': Duane Dibbley
(Danny John-Jules) and the Doyle brothers (Chris Barrie and Craig Charles) in
'Back to Reality' (Photographer: Mike Vaughan)

The indestructible Starbug – crashed more times than a ZX81
(Photographer: Paul Grant)

'Maybe a little synaptic enhancer will do the trick': Lister (Craig Charles)
and Kryten (Robert Llewellyn) in 'Psirens' (Photographer: Mike Vaughan)

ever to be in a position where he might endanger the crew? A man so petty and small-minded he would while away his evenings sewing name labels on to his ship-issue condoms? A man of such awesome stupidity . . .

RIMMER: Objection . . .

JUSTICE COMPUTER: Objection overruled.

KRYTEN: A man of such awesome stupidity, he even objects to his own defence counsel. An over-zealous, trumped-up little squirt . . .

RIMMER: Objection.

JUSTICE COMPUTER: Overruled.

KRYTEN: An incompetent vending-machine repairman with a Napoleon complex, who commanded as much respect and affection from his fellow crew members as Long John Silver's parrot . . .

RIMMER: Objection.

JUSTICE COMPUTER: If you object to your own counsel once more, Mr Rimmer, you'll be in contempt.

KRYTEN: Who would put this man, this joke of a man, a man who couldn't outwit a used tea bag, in a position of authority where he could wipe out an entire crew? Who? Only a yoghurt. This man is not guilty of manslaughter. He's only guilty of being Arnold J. Rimmer. That is his crime. It is also his punishment. Defence rests.

He sits down next to Rimmer, and stares fixidly ahead. RIMMER *shoots him a little look, not quite sure what to think.*

JUSTICE COMPUTER: The defendant will stand for the verdict.

RIMMER *stands.*

JUSTICE COMPUTER: In view of your counsel's eloquent defence, together with the reams of material evidence he submitted on computer card, this court accepts that, in your case, the mind-probe is not an adequate method of ascertaining guilt. It is not possible for you to have committed the crimes for which you blame yourself, and you may therefore go free.

RIMMER: Objection!

KRYTEN: Sir, what are you objecting to?

RIMMER: I want an apology.

17. Int. Starbug rear

KRYTEN *and* RIMMER *come up the ramp, followed by* LISTER *and* CAT.

RIMMER: Brilliant, Kryten. What can I say? You were brilliant. You even had me believing it. The way you twisted the facts and made them seem to fit that pattern.

CAT: Come on, let's get out of here. I don't know what made us want to come to this hell-hole in the first place.

LISTER: I do.

They all look at the pod. It is open. And it's empty.

CAT: (*Smiles*) Can I smell perfume?

The SIMULANT *lurches into the doorway from the cockpit area, brandishing a bazookoid and an evil-looking handgun.*

SIMULANT: I doubt it.

LISTER *grabs a bazookoid by the door and starts backing out.*

CAT: Are you by any chance Barbra Bellini? I didn't think so.

18. Int. Corridor on colony

Red Dwarf crew fleeing down corridor.

CAT: To think I caressed his pod!

They leap over the escort boots and run on.

19. Same corridor on colony

The SIMULANT *running along. A pair of escort boots shuffles towards him. He blasts the left one. The right boot turns and starts hopping for its life. The* SIMULANT *takes careful aim and blasts it in the back of the heel.*

20. Int. Another corridor on the colony

The CREW *race under the archway bathed in a strange light.*

JUSTICE COMPUTER: You are now entering the Justice Zone. Beyond this point, it is impossible to commit any act of injustice.

LISTER *and* RIMMER *dash off one way.* CAT *and* KRYTEN *go the other.*

21. Int. Corridor on colony

SIMULANT *walking along, looking for them.*

SIMULANT: Hey, my friends, I don't want any trouble. I just want your space craft. Give me the start-up code. Look! (*Holds up his gun.*) I have no weapon. (*Throws gun aside.*)

Cut to: RIMMER *and* LISTER *on metal walkway. As he walks under them* LISTER *has the* SIMULANT *in his sights.*

RIMMER: What are you waiting for? Gloop him.
LISTER: I can't. He's not armed.
RIMMER: Lister, this isn't a Scout meeting. We're not trying to win the Best-Behaved Troop flag. Gloop him.
LISTER: What? In the back?
RIMMER: Of course in the back. It's only a pity he's awake.
LISTER: You mean you could happily kill him if he was asleep?
RIMMER: I could happily kill him if he was on the job. Gloop him.

LISTER: It's immoral.

SIMULANT: Come on, you wouldn't shoot an unarmed droid. Come out and let's discuss it.

LISTER *sets aside his gun.*

LISTER: I'm going to talk to him.

22. Int. Metal gangway

SIMULANT *stands, unarmed, as* LISTER *drops into shot.*

LISTER: You want to talk? Let's talk.

SIMULANT: You have no weapon?

LISTER: No. You have no weapon?

SIMULANT: No.

They walk towards each other.

SIMULANT: Guess what? (*Pulls out hunting knife.*) I lied.

LISTER: Guess what? (*Allows pole to slide from the arm of his jacket.*) So did I.

SIMULANT: But I lied twice. (*Pulls out a handgun.*)

LISTER: I didn't think of that.

SIMULANT: I'm very glad you didn't.

LISTER: What did you want to talk about?

SIMULANT: Your death. (*Cocks the gun.*) Your imminent death.

Fires at Lister's chest. LISTER *looks down at his chest. There's no wound. The* SIMULANT *fires again. Still no wound. And again. No wound. Suddenly three bullet wounds appear in the Simulant's chest. He staggers forwards, bewildered.* LISTER *hits the Simulant over the head with his pole. Then* LISTER *reels back, dazed and half-conscious and falls to his knees. The* SIMULANT *fires again. Another bullet wound appears in the Simulant's body, this time in his shoulder.* LISTER *staggers to his feet, swings the club again, sideways, catching the Simulant in the midriff, but it's* LISTER *who feels the impact of the blow and flies out of shot. He is lying in a crumpled heap.*

LISTER: What the smeg is going on?

The SIMULANT *looks at his gun, casts it aside. Staggers a bit. Takes out the knife again and hurls it at* LISTER. *The dagger appears in the Simulant's chest. He pulls it out, slightly bemused, and hurls it at* LISTER *again. This time, it appears in the Simulant's head.* LISTER *grins. Enlightenment spreads over his features. He grabs a nearby bottle and hands it to the staggering* SIMULANT.

SIMULANT: Zzzzzt. Does not compute. Zzzzzt. Error. Zzzzzt. Malfunction.

SIMULANT *smashes it over Lister's head. The* SIMULANT *staggers and shakes his head.* LISTER *hands more bottles to the Simulant, who smashes them over Lister's head, staggering and growling with each blow. Finally,* LISTER *grabs the Simulant's hands, puts them around his neck, and the* SIMULANT *tries to throttle him but, obviously, is really strangling himself. Nearly choking to death, he releases his grip and staggers back.* LISTER *takes out an indelible pen and marks a target on his groin. He walks towards the almost beaten Simulant, thrusting his groin forward as he goes. The* SIMULANT *kicks Lister in the groin.* LISTER *stands there, grinning, as the* SIMULANT *flies backwards and collapses into a defeated heap. The* CAT *runs up brandishing a huge snow shovel.*

CAT: I've got him, buddy. Leave this to me.
LISTER: Cat! No!
CAT: Better late than never.

CAT *raises the shovel high above his head, and slams the* SIMULANT *over the head. The* CAT *laughs triumphantly. Suddenly, the smile freezes on his face, and he falls backwards out of shot.*

23. Model shot. Starbug landing in Red Dwarf cargo bay

24. Int. Red Dwarf corridor. Day

LISTER, RIMMER, KRYTEN *and* CAT, *walking back.*

LISTER: Makes you think, doesn't it? Mankind's history has been one long search for justice. That's what all religions are about: they accept life as being basically unfair but promise everyone will get their just deserts later: heaven, hell, karma, reincarnation, whatever. Those guys who built that penal colony tried to give some order to the universe by creating the Justice Field. But when you're living in an environment where justice does exist, there's no free will. That's why in our universe there can never be true, natural justice – good things will happen to bad people, and bad things will happen to good people. It's the way it's got to be. Life, by its very nature, has to be cruel, unkind and unfair.

LISTER *falls down an open manhole cover.*

CAT: Thank god for that.

CAT *puts the lid on, and they walk off.*

BACK TO REALITY

1. Model shot
Eerie music. Underwater. An ocean bed. Strange, unfamiliar flora and fauna abound. No fish. We see Starbug on the ocean bed, close to the wreck of a crashed spaceship, the SSS Esperanto.

2. PR–VT. Int. Crashed vessel. Moody
The ship has been here for some time. Water drips from various pipes. There is a film of water on the floor. It's so dark and gloomy, we can't make out much more.

The CAT, LISTER *and* KRYTEN *appear from around a corner in their diving suits with bright torches and begin cautiously walking down the corridor.* KRYTEN *spots a terminal on the bulkhead.*

3. Int. Starbug cockpit. Undersea
RIMMER *is hunched over a monitor, which is relaying shots from Lister's POV.*

KRYTEN: (*Fzzt*) Mr Rimmer, sir. We've located the black-box terminal. You should be getting something now . .

RIMMER *glances at the computer monitor. Details are being printed on screen.*

RIMMER: Confirmed. Ident details: SSS *Esperanto* . . . Ocean seeding ship . . .

4. PR–VT. Int. Crashed vessel. Moody

CAT, KRYTEN *and* LISTER *continue to explore, cautiously. Over, we hear:*

RIMMER: (*VO – dist*) Mission: to introduce oceanic life to potential S3 planets ... This was a recon trip ... a three-year check ... strictly routine, to make sure the amino-acid chain had taken ... They'd been trying out some new enhancement technique to accelerate the evolutionary process. Topped even their best projections. They got five million years of evolution in three solar years.

KRYTEN: (*Fzzt – whistles.*)

CAT: (*Fzzt*) So what happened to them?

5. Int. Starbug cockpit. Undersea

RIMMER *reading from screen:*

RIMMER: Final entry: routine stuff. They spent the day cataloguing and indexing the new life forms ... Then it stops.

6. PR–VT. Int. Crashed vessel. Moody

KRYTEN: (*Fzzt*) A question that occurs: if this ocean is supposed to be teeming with new life forms, where are they all?

LISTER: (*Fzzt*) What are you implying, Kryten?

KRYTEN: (*Fzzt*) No implication intended, sir.

LISTER: (*Fzzt*) You're saying there's some huge great damn fish out there, aren't you? Some kind of gigantic prehistoric leviathan who's porked its way through this entire ocean.

KRYTEN: (*Fzzt*) That is one option.

LISTER: (*Fzzt*) Any alternatives?

KRYTEN: (*Fzzt*) None that occur.

CAT: (*Fzzt*) Wait a minute – I've got it. Don't fish swim south for the winter?

KRYTEN: (*Fzzt*) No, that's birds, sir.

CAT: (*Fzzt*) Birds swim south for the winter? How do they breathe?

LISTER *has wandered up the corridor and found something.*

LISTER: (*Fzzt*) Guys. Rimmer – are you getting this?

7. Int. Starbug cockpit. Undersea

RIMMER *is looking at Lister's POV monitor.* LISTER *has found a dead crew member, a skeleton in a space suit.*

RIMMER: Got it. Looks like Norman Bates's mum.

KRYTEN *comes into Lister's POV and runs his psi-scan over the corpse.*

KRYTEN: (*Fzzt*) Human. Male. Caucasian. Cause of death: gunshot wound to the head. From the entry and exit wounds, most likely self-inflicted.

KRYTEN *indicates the gun, still clasped in the skeleton's gauntlet.*

CAT: (*VO – Fzzt*) There's another one . . .

8. PR–VT. Int. Crashed vessel. Moody

The CAT *is standing before a hanged space-suited skeleton dangling from a ceiling joist.* KRYTEN *is scanning.*

LISTER: (*Fzzt*) Two suicides?
CAT: (*Fzzt*) There's more!

9. Int. Starbug cockpit. Undersea

RIMMER *looking at Lister's POV as he swings round to the Cat. Yet another skeletal astronaut, who has clearly committed hara-kiri.*

KRYTEN: (*Fzzt*) Male . . . Oriental. Clearly, he has committed seppuku.

CAT: (*Fzzt*) Hey. Look what I found.

LISTER *turns to the Cat, who is holding a dead fish.*

10. PR–VT. Int. Crashed vessel. Moody
KRYTEN *scans the fish.*

KRYTEN: (*Fzzt*) Species unknown. Similar to Earth haddock. Cause of death – suffocation.

KRYTEN *spots a strange readout and taps the psi-scan.*

RIMMER: What is it?

KRYTEN: (*Fzzt*) This fish suffocated in water – it voluntarily closed its own gills.

CAT: (*Fzzt*) Are you saying this haddock committed suicide?

KRYTEN: (*Fzzt*) I am merely stating the known facts. This fish relinquished its life of its own free will. Damn fool.

LISTER: (*Fzzt*) Why would a haddock kill itself? Why am I even asking that question?

CAT: (*Fzzt*) Hold it, hang five, guys, I'm getting something. (*Indicates the corpses.*) He committed suicide, he committed suicide, he committed suicide and the fish committed suicide: there's some kind of link here that I can't quite put my finger on.

LISTER *is crouching by a pool of green liquid.*

LISTER: (*Fzzt*) Hang on a minute, guys, check this.

KRYTEN *runs the psi-scan over the liquid.*

KRYTEN: (*Fzzt*) It's an unknown compound. Best guess: some kind of hallucinogenic venom, secreted by a piscine source, not unlike an Earth octopus or giant squid.

LISTER: (*Fzzt*) So this is octopus ink?

KRYTEN: (*Fzzt*) I'm just completing the chemical analysis. Ah. Oh. We have answers.

LISTER: (*Fzzt*) What? What?

KRYTEN: (*Fzzt*) Oh, yes, uhm, ahhh, well ... No, wait ...
Ermmm ... Yes. No. Better still ... Yes. Uh, suh, sir, I
am invoking Space Corps directive 1947945, which clearly
states that a mechanoid may issue orders to human crew
members if the lives of said crew members are directly or
indirectly under threat from a hitherto unperceived source
and there is inadequate time to explain the precise nature of
the enormous and most imminent ... yes, terribly imminent, death threat. Under these conditions I am therefore em-
powered to issue the order. (*In the same tone*) Get the hell
out of here.

LISTER: (*Fzzt*) I'm history.

11. Int. Starbug cockpit. Undersea

*Shot: Lister's POV monitor, shooting the floor as he runs towards
the airlock.*

RIMMER: Kryten, what's going on?

KRYTEN: (*Fzzt*) Entering airlock ...

Lister's boots jump into the airlock. We hear airlock door close.

LISTER: (*Fzzt*) Repressurizing now.

12. PR-VT. Int. Repressurization chamber

LISTER, KRYTEN *and* CAT *as the chamber fills with water.*

KRYTEN: (*Fzzt*) Some kind of sea creature – a life form we've
never encountered before – attacked this ship. Its defence
mechanism is a curious one. It secretes a venom, possibly
even an hallucinogenic, which dysfunctions its prey by
inducing despair. That's why all the crew and even that fish
committed suicide... Unfortunately, we have been contami-
nated ourselves. It's a greatly reduced dose, but we can expect
... (*Whimpers.*) ... bouts of total despair and anguish.

RIMMER: (*VO*) What about Lister and the Cat?

LISTER: I'm OK. I don't seem to be affected. It's true, I don't think anyone's ever truly loved me in my entire life, but, uh . . . (*Whimpers.*) . . . there's nothing new about that.

KRYTEN *and* LISTER *start blubbering quietly.*

CAT: What's gotten into you guys? This is like Saturday night at the Wailing Wall. Why is it always me who has to be the strong one? (*Starts sobbing.*) Without me, you guys'd just fall apart.

KRYTEN: We should get back as soon as we can (*Blubs*) and take a mood-stabilizer – suggest lithium carbonate.

13. Int. Starbug cockpit. Undersea

RIMMER: Uh, I know, emotionally, this probably isn't the news you want to hear right now, but there's a blob on the sonar scope the size of New Mexico, and it's heading your way.

HOLLY: I think our friend the suicide squid is about to make an appearance.

KRYTEN: (*VO*) Where is it precisely?

RIMMER: Directly above you, about two thousand fathoms and diving.

LISTER: (*VO* – *whimpering*) Oh, thanks a lot, Rimmer. You know the state we're in, and you have to go and give us news like that. You couldn't have lied?

RIMMER: I was lying – it's only one thousand fathoms.

14. Model shot
Starbug *on ocean bed, as the divers head towards it. Suddenly it is covered by a huge shadow.*

15. Int. Starbug cockpit. Undersea

LISTER *and the* CAT, *half-unsuited, are breathing through oxygen masks connected to lithium carbonate cylinders. Together with* RIMMER *and* KRYTEN, *they are looking at the sonar as the blob lies static above them.*

RIMMER: What's it doing?

LISTER: It's trying to work out what we are. Cut power.

KRYTEN *flips switches. Lights go out. The only sound is the blip-blip of* Starbug's *sonar.*

RIMMER: This venom. Are we safe in here?

LISTER: It penetrated the hull of Class D Space Corps seeding ship. In comparison, we're a sardine tin.

RIMMER: It's moving.

LISTER: Where?

RIMMER: Down.

LISTER: Speed?

HOLLY: Fifteen knots, sixteen, eighteen . . .

RIMMER: It's diving.

LISTER: Course?

HOLLY: Collision.

KRYTEN: Do we move or stay?

HOLLY: Twenty-five knots . . . Thirty-five . . . fifty.

RIMMER: It's coming straight for us.

LISTER: There are only three options. It thinks we're a threat, food or a mate. It's going to kill us, eat us or hump us. We either persuade it we're not that kind of oceanic salvage vessel or we scarper, pronto.

CAT: Are you out of your mind? To be diddled by a giant squid – on a first date? Think how we'd feel in the morning.

LISTER: We're going to try and outrun it. Holly, hit the power and give me manual.

16. Model shot
Under the growing shadow of the diving leviathan, Starbug *comes to life and blasts off the ocean bed.*

17. Int. Starbug cockpit. Undersea
Starbug *is accelerating.* LISTER *and* KRYTEN *are piloting. Shot of the sonar: 'Squid' is closing.*

18. Model sequence
Starbug *is cutting through the water, chased by the 'Squid' (we see as little of the sea creature as possible – shadows, details) over the ocean bed, between rocks and coral formations.* Starbug *clips rocks. Detail: A tentacle rips off one of* Starbug's *landing legs.*

19. Int. Starbug cockpit. Undersea
Concentration. LISTER *steering.*

HOLLY: Change bearing – one-zero-five. There're some natural caverns, about three klicks away – might give us some cover.
KRYTEN: Acknowledged, Holly. New course, set.

20. Model shot
Detail: the 'Squid' ejaculates its 'ink'. Starbug *running away from the growing cloud of ink. The ink hits.*

21. Int. Starbug cockpit. Undersea

LISTER: It's hit us.
RIMMER: Look out!

22. Model shot
Starbug *smashes into a cliff face.*

23. Int. Starbug cockpit. Undersea

In slow motion: shards of glass are hurled towards them as Starbug's *windshield implodes.*

24. Model shot

Starbug *explodes and everyone is killed, so we need an explosion that is so complete no one could possibly have survived it. We see debris sink to the ocean bed, including Kryten's head and maybe the odd limb or two. Hugely sad music as we track Kryten's dead head to the bottom. At this point the music changes to an upbeat electronic arcade-game version of the* Red Dwarf *theme, and we mix to . . .*

25. Graphics

LISTER , KRYTEN, RIMMER *and the* CAT *as computer sprites.*

LISTER SPRITE: Is it just me, or did everything suddenly become two-dimensional?

CAT SPRITE: What's happening?

RIMMER SPRITE: Kryten? Any theories?

KRYTEN SPRITE: My psi-scan does not appear to be functioning.

Over their heads, the giant letters 'GAME OVER' appear. They all look up.

CAT SPRITE: I have a very bad feeling about this.

RIMMER SPRITE: Oh, my God . . .

LISTER SPRITE: This can't be happening.

KRYTEN SPRITE: I'm afraid it is, sir.

And we mix from graphics to:

26. Int. Gaming Booth. Day

LISTER, RIMMER, KRYTEN *and the* CAT *in the same position but connected to some computer banks by VR-ish helmets, suits, feed tubes, etc. They are all sitting in what look like racing-car seats, in separated booths, much like those in arcade sit-down games, only they face outwards and are covered with bio-feedback devices, massage machines, etc. − everything they need to sustain them while they play the game.*

They all sit there, more than a little gob-smacked. Through wall speakers, we hear:

WOMAN'S VOICE: For the last four years, you have been engaged in the Total Immersion Video game 'Red Dwarf'. As with all role-playing adventures, you will experience a certain amount of disorientation on leaving the game. It will be several minutes before your real-life memories return, so, in the meantime, please disengage the game-playing machinery and relax until an attendant is free to answer any of your questions. On behalf of Leisure World International may we be the first to say, welcome back to reality.

They start to disengage the machinery, ripping Velcro connections and bio-feedback devices off their clothes. They are wearing thin white boiler suits with bare feet. They are all wide-eyed and completely disoriented. They mutter incredulities. RIMMER *is no longer a hologram.* KRYTEN *is no longer a mechanoid but a cyberzoid − he has a human body and some high-tech electronic add-ons to his mask, which is topped by a metal skull plate. The overall effect is of a mechanized human. The* CAT *is a klutz. He is clumsy and gauche. He has a Jerry Lewis nutty-professor over-bite.*

LISTER: This is a very, very bad dream, right?
RIMMER: (*Flatly*) I'm not a hologram.
KRYTEN: I'm half human.
CAT: (*Feeling his mouth*) What the hell's happened to my teeth? I can open beer bottles with my overbite.

The door opens and the attendant, ANDY *(a blue-collar, mechanic type), comes in and starts to re-set the machines.*

ANDY: All right, lads? How're you feeling? Bit wonky? It's perfectly normal. You'll be right as rain in twenty minutes. So if you could just move through to the Recuperation Lounge, I can get things ready for the next lot.

LISTER: The next lot?

ANDY: Very popular game, Red Dwarf. Got a two-year waiting list. Well, we've only got twenty machines. So, how did you get killed then?

KRYTEN: Some kind of squid.

ANDY: Oh! The despair squid — there's no way that should kill you. Why didn't you use the laser cannons? It's obvious.

KRYTEN: *Starbug* doesn't ... didn't possess a laser-cannon capability.

ANDY: You twonk! You use the laser cannons on the crashed whatsit, the *Esperanto*. That's how you get out of it.

RIMMER: How ... how on Earth were we supposed to know that, you Brummie git?

ANDY: *Esperanto*. It's a clue, innit? *Esperanto*. Hope. Hope defeats despair. The despair squid. It's a blatant clue. Bla-tant. Bloomin' heck, if you didn't get that, you must have been playing like puddings. Who was playing Lister?

LISTER: Me.

ANDY: Did you get Kochanski?

LISTER: Was I supposed to?

ANDY: Supposed to? It's the objective of the game for Lister, you twonk. You're separated to begin with, then it's basically a love story across time, space, death and reality. You must have got the easy stuff, though. What did you think of the planet of the Nymphomaniacs?

RIMMER: The planet of the what?

ANDY: You missed that? Oh — it's a riot, that is. Some people spend years on that. Which one was Rimmer?

RIMMER: (*Smiles in a what-an-asshole-he-was kind of way*) Ah. Me.

ANDY: He's amazing, isn't he?

RIMMER: You can say that again.

ANDY: How long did it take you to suss him out then?

RIMMER: Oh, I had him sussed from the beginning.

ANDY: Really? You found the Captain's message right away?

RIMMER: What Captain's message?

ANDY: The one that's hidden in the microdot of the 'i' in Rimmer's swimming certificate. Well, that's the clue, isn't it? Rimmer having a swimming certificate and yet not being able to swim.

KRYTEN: And that's a clue?

ANDY: Yeah. It's a blatant clue, isn't it?

RIMMER: A blatant clue to what?

ANDY: A blatant clue to the truth behind Rimmer.

RIMMER: What truth?

ANDY: Coh! How long did you play this game? The truth as to why he's such an insufferable prat!

RIMMER: It's because of his parents. And his upbringing, and his background, and the fact he was never loved . . .

ANDY: No, no, no.

RIMMER: Yes, yes, yes.

ANDY: No, no, no.

RIMMER: Yes, yes, yes, yes.

ANDY: NO!

RIMMER: WHAT WAS IT THEN?

ANDY: He was a hand-picked special agent for the Space Corps. He'd had his memory erased and was programmed to act like a complete twonk so no one would suspect he was on a secret mission to destroy Red Dwarf, in order to guide Lister to his destiny as creator of the second Universe.

LISTER: You what?

ANDY: Yeah, you know. That bit where Lister jump-starts the second Big Bang with jump leads from *Starbug*.

RIMMER: Jump-starts the second Big Bang?

ANDY: Yeah. Well, that's it isn't it? The final irony: Lister, who is the ultimate atheist, turns out, in fact, to be God.

LISTER: You what?

ANDY: It's all in the Captain's message. It's all in the microdot. (*A thought occurs to him. He turns to Rimmer.*) Wait a minute – are you seriously telling me that you were playing the prat version of Rimmer all the time? For four years? That's classic. Classic.

Four fairly good-looking, well-built guys come in. These are the new Red Dwarf *players. (Are you worried yet, guys?)*

ANDY: All right, lads. Which one's Lister?

NEW LISTER *holds his hand up.* LISTER *looks him up and down, critically.*

ANDY: Right. (*He indicates Lister's booth.*) Food bag, bio-feedback, catheter. It's all there. Start plugging yourself in. Whatever you do, don't mix up the food pipe with the catheter. One guy did that – we didn't spot it for days. (*Laughs.*) OK, Kryten, in you go, son.

NEW RIMMER *moves towards the booth.*

ANDY: (*Indicates booths*) Cat, Rimmer . . .

The old crew stand there, looking sad and lost.

ANDY: (*To old crew*) Here give us a bit of room, will you, chaps?

KRYTEN: Whu-where do we go? We don't know who we are. Our memories haven't returned yet.

ANDY: The Recuperation Lounge. I keep telling you. Blimey, no wonder you only scored 4 per cent.

They shuffle out sadly.

ANDY: What a bunch of twonks.

27. Int. Recuperation room. Day

A clean but downmarket waiting room with sofas and a large coffee table with magazines on it. Food- and drink-vending machines, a TV set. They all sit around, looking miserable.

LISTER: I'm not Lister, then. I'm not me, am I?

KRYTEN: None of us are who we thought we were, sir. This is going to take some getting used to.

RIMMER: I'm not Rimmer, then?

KRYTEN: No.

RIMMER: I'm not a hologram. (*Smiles broadly.*) I'm not Rimmer. (*Brays delightedly.*)

CAT: But if we're not who we thought we were, who the hell are we?

LISTER: We're the kind of sad acts who want to spend four years playing a computer game. Either we're running away from God knows what or we've got nothing worth living for in the first place.

They all look at the floor for a while. The door opens, and an ORDERLY *pops her head in.*

ORDERLY: Is there a Duane Dibbley in here?

LISTER: Pardon?

ORDERLY: Duane Dibbley.

LISTER: No. Sorry.

The ORDERLY *goes.*

RIMMER: (*To* LISTER) Wait a minute – how d'you know there's no one here called Duane Dibbley? It could be you.

The ORDERLY *comes in, carrying a long-term storage case, large enough for clothes, etc.*

ORDERLY: No, this is right. Dibbley. This is the Dibbley party. Which one's Duane Dibbley?

They all sit there, hoping it's not them. Then, as one, they turn and look at the Cat.

CAT: No.

The ORDERLY *looks at the photo on the ID ticket.*

CAT: No. Please no. I don't want to be Duane Dibbley.

The ORDERLY *looks at him.*

ORDERLY: It's you. Here are your party's clothes and possessions. The medical officer will be down in twenty minutes.

The ORDERLY *puts Dibbley's case on the table and goes.*

CAT: (*Sobbing silently*) Duane Dibbley. How can I be called Duane Dibbley?

LISTER: (*Reading the ID tag*) It's true – it's got your photograph, name and address and everything. (*Opens the case and rummages through.*) There's an anorak in here . . .

Stay on the Cat's reaction.

LISTER: . . . White socks . . . nylon shirt . . . plastic sandals . . . aertex vest . . . cardigan . . . Oh, and a key to the Salvation Army hostel . . .

CAT: It doesn't make sense.

RIMMER: I'm sorry, but I'm afraid it makes perfect sense . . . Duane. Imagine a guy with no élan, no style, a misfit. Doesn't it make total sense that this hapless creature would give his back teeth to play someone like the Cat in a computer game?

CAT: So this is really me: a no-style gimbo with teeth the Druids could use as a place of worship.

RIMMER: Kryten (*Flicks fingers*), open the next one.

KRYTEN: (*Wheels round*) Listen, whoever you are: don't push your luck by ordering whoever I am around, because, whoever I am, I'm almost certainly not the kind of guy who takes crap from whoever you are (*Jabbing his finger at Rimmer*). So before you order me about, let's establish if

I'm the kind of guy who doesn't mind being ordered around, or I'm the kind of guy who gets uptight being ordered around by the kind of guy you are. Clear?

RIMMER: All I said was 'Open the next one.'

LISTER *is reading the label on the next case.*

LISTER: (*To* KRYTEN) This one's you.

KRYTEN: Who . . . who am I?

LISTER: (*Flips open the case*) Wow. You're a detective in the Cybernautic Division of the Police Department.

KRYTEN *can't conceal his pride.*

KRYTEN: Golly. Really?

LISTER: Yeah, this is your badge.

KRYTEN: (*Toughening up*) A detective, huh? What's my name?

LISTER: 'Jake' . . . 'Jake Bullet'.

KRYTEN: Jake Bullet — Cybernautic Detective. I like that. Sounds like the kind of hard-living flatfoot who gets the job done by cutting corners and bucking authority. And if those pen-pushers up at City Hall don't like it, they can park their over-paid, fat asses on this mid digit and swivel till they squeal like pigs on honeymoon.

RIMMER: On the other hand, Mr Bullet, perhaps the Cybernautics Division is in charge of traffic control and you just happen to have a rather silly macho name.

KRYTEN: Oh, yes, sir. Good point. I didn't think of that.

CAT: (*Shaking his head*) Duane Dibbley.

RIMMER: (*To* LISTER) So, whoever you are. Who's next?

LISTER: I don't want to know. Someone else look.

KRYTEN: Stand aside. Let the Law handle this. (*Reads label*) No photograph. Name, 'Billy Doyle'.

Everyone looks at LISTER.

LISTER: Not necessarily. It's not necessarily me.

LISTER *goes to the case and pulls out a disgusting, dirty greatcoat. Lonely from 'Callan' passed this coat down to Rigsby; he threw it out and now it's here.*

RIMMER: Billy Doyle. Well, there's a name that's come from the wrong side of the tracks. You can see it all, can't you? A youth spent in and out of corrective institutions. A string of illegitimate children. The wife'll be all white shoes, no tights and blotchy legs. Has to take up petty crime to cover the court orders for maintenance. Before he knows it, he's standing in a bank with a sawn-off shotgun. Somehow it goes off. An old lady gets both barrels through her crocheted bobble hat. All he can do is hide. But where? Then it hits him: with his ill-gotten gains he can buy four years in a computer game and wait till the heat's off. So ends the ballad of Billy 'Granny-killer' Doyle.

LISTER: (*Proffering coat to Rimmer*) It's yours.

RIMMER: What?

LISTER: It's yours . . . Bill.

RIMMER: No.

LISTER: Check out the ugly mug on the ID, man.

RIMMER: (*Reads ID*) William Doyle. (*Rolls it around a bit*) William . . . Doyle. Good old Bill Doyle. You know, that sounds like a hell of a good name to me. Probably connected with the Boston Doyles. Old money, blue-chip stock . . . You know, I think it's all coming back now.

LISTER: The thing that puzzles me slightly is what a man of such undoubted good breeding is doing with a coat which smells like an elderly male yak has taken a leak in both the pockets.

RIMMER: Well, isn't it obvious?

KRYTEN: No, it isn't.

As RIMMER *speaks, he is rooting through his belongings, producing clothes of unfathomable filthiness – a holey cardigan, a shirt with the collar almost detached, some fingerless mittens, huge, yellow stained underpants . . .*

RIMMER: Of course it is, Jake. Just think about it: William Doyle IV, heir to the Doyle billions, strolling home from another masquerade ball, his hover limo gliding along twenty yards in front, when suddenly a gang of working-class people attack him from behind. They beat him, strip him naked, dress him in this disgusting outfit and dump him, unconscious, in a computer-game arcade, where no one will think of looking for him. Don't you see? Isn't that totally, totally, totally credible? (*Suddenly crumbles*) Oh, my God! My names's Billy Doyle, and my cologne is Eau de Yak Urine.

LISTER: So who am I then?

LISTER *has opened his case and is sorting through some very sober but expensive-looking clothes.*

LISTER: This stuff is really, really expensive.

RIMMER: Are you quite, absolutely, sure that isn't my box?

KRYTEN: Who are you? What do you do?

LISTER: Work for some company ... CGI. I've got a limo in the long-term car park.

LISTER *is pulling out expensive paraphernalia – watches, cigar cases, etc.*

RIMMER: Well. Clearly, you've been privy to all the breaks and advantages life denied poor old William Doyle here.

KRYTEN: Sir, I think you should take a look at this. (*Holds out Lister's ID card.*) William, meet your brother, Sebastian.

RIMMER *and* LISTER *are stunned.*

KRYTEN: Well, half-brothers. Uterinal. Same mother.

28. Int. Corridor. Day

A corridor in the game emporium. LISTER, RIMMER, KRYTEN *and the* CAT *file past camera. In their street clothes now, they are heading for the car park. There is a viewing window set into one of the walls.* KRYTEN *is wearing a long trench coat. The* CAT *is in his anorak, too-short trousers and white socks, clutching a plastic bag to his chest. His shoes squeak loudly with every step.*

KRYTEN: This is a crazy idea. We can't leave now – our memories haven't returned yet.

RIMMER: We've got to find out more about ourselves. I refuse to accept I'm his alky, drop-out, yak-coat-wearing half-brother.

CAT: Duane Dibbley?

As the others walk on, LISTER *stops and looks into the viewing window. Inside we see:*

29. Int. Starbug cockpit. Romantic

NEW LISTER, *in a battle-stained white vest, oiled muscles and a bandana on his head, is driving* Starbug, *a huge, half-smoked, now unlit cigar in the corner of his mouth. Behind them is the macho* NEW RIMMER, *and the* NEW CAT, *more of a lion, warrior-like and ferocious.* KRYTEN *is a bald human in a mechanoid suit. Suddenly the beautiful* NEW KOCHANSKI *storms in from the airlock.*

NEW KOCHANSKI: (*Angry*) Are you crazy, Lister? Are you totally nuts? You risked your own neck and everybody else's just to save my life. Do that again, and I'll kill you!

NEW LISTER: Kochanski?

NEW KOCHANSKI: What?

NEW LISTER *grabs her with one hand by the lapels and pulls her towards him.*

NEW LISTER: Shaddup.

He spits out his cigar and kisses her. She beats his shoulders with her hands, but then not a cliché is unturned as she slowly surrenders to his appalling macho-ness.

30. Int. Arcade corridor. Day

LISTER *looks up and gives a little thin smile to disguise his jealousy, then follows the others.*

Pre–VT. Ext. Underground car park. Day

A broken, dirty sign over the lift reads 'Leisure World International Total Immersion Videos Arcade'. LISTER, RIMMER, KRYTEN *and the* CAT *emerge. By the lift, a political poster reads: 'Vote Fascist – for a third glorious decade of total law enforcement'. Next to it: 'Be a government informer – betray your family and friends. Fabulous prizes to be won!' They exchange looks.*

Pre–VT. Ext. Underground car park. Day

They walk up to a superb limo, Cat's shoes still squeaking.

RIMMER: This is your car?
LISTER: (*Checks ticket on his car keys*) Bay 47.

As LISTER *moves to open the car, we hear a voice, off:*

COP: (*VO*) Halt or I fire!

An URCHIN GIRL, *clutching a fresh green apple, dashes through Cat, Rimmer and Kryten and runs off. The* COP *raises his weapon in their direction.*

COP: Move, voters!

They stand there. As RIMMER *makes to move:*

KRYTEN: (*Through gritted teeth to Rimmer*) Move one inch, and I'll crush every bone in your body.

We see the URCHIN *escape. The* COP *goes up to them.*

COP: You helped an enemy of democracy to escape. She was stealing an apple of the people.
KRYTEN: (*Flashes badge*) Bullet. Cybernautics.

COP: That's traffic control.

KRYTEN: It is? Oh, I . . . sorry.

COP: (*Trains gun on them*) Kneel, voters, you are under sentence of death.

As he cocks his gun, he hears LISTER *scuffle, wheels round and trains his gun on him.*

COP: Come out of the shadows, voter.

LISTER: (*Hands up*) What's the beef? Did she steal your lunch box?

The COP *double-takes, drops his gun to his side and salutes.*

COP: Many, many apologies, voter Colonel. Had I known it was you . . .

He snaps his heels together.

COP: Forgive me.

They all look at LISTER.

LISTER: You know me?

COP: Of course, voter Colonel.

LISTER: Who am I?

COP: You are Colonel Sebastian Doyle, section chief of the CGI, head of the Ministry of Alteration.

LISTER: Remind me. What exactly do we do at the Ministry of Alteration?

COP: You . . . change people, voter Colonel.

LISTER: In what way?

COP: You change them from being alive people into being dead people. To purify democracy.

RIMMER: Purify?

COP: No one has done more to purge the ballot boxes of bad voters than the voter Colonel.

KRYTEN: So why has he been away four years?

COP: Excuse me, voter Colonel – but is this some kind of test?

LISTER: Answer him.

COP: The rumour was you had . . . grown weary of your . . . glorious duties and had gone away in secret to . . . renew yourself.

CAT, KRYTEN and RIMMER look at LISTER. We hear a whimper. The COP turns and spots the URCHIN GIRL sneaking for the exit. He drops into firing stance, and levels his weapon at the urchin.

COP: Halt!

COP smiles. Stay on his smile as we hear six shots. The COP drops down, dead, revealing KRYTEN behind him, holding a smoking gun. They all stand, frozen in shock. Off, we hear a distant siren start to wail. LISTER, CAT and KRYTEN unfreeze and make hastily for the limo. KRYTEN is still in shock.

31. Int. Starbug rear. Undersea

They all stand in their diving outfits, in the same positions as they were in the car park. KRYTEN is holding a smoking flare gun.

KRYTEN: I killed him.

LISTER: There's no time for that – get in the car!

LISTER mimes opening the driver's door.

KRYTEN: I killed a human.

CAT: In the car!

The CAT opens the imaginary car door and sits in the imaginary back seat, next to RIMMER, who is fastening an imaginary seat belt. LISTER grabs KRYTEN and stuffs him in the passenger seat, then runs round the imaginary bonnet and jumps into the driver's seat.

RIMMER: (*Looking out of the 'window'*) Look out – Fascist cops by the lifts, and they're armed!

LISTER *starts up the car, and with a lunge they all mime pulling off, ducking gunfire.* RIMMER *looks round at the Cat's arm.*

RIMMER: You're hit!

The CAT *looks down at his arm and clutches his imaginary wound.* HOLLY *on the monitor is wearily watching the action.*

HOLLY: (*Eyes closed – she's been trying to get through for hours*) Hello – for the three thousandth time – you're hallucinating. Can anyone hear me?

LISTER *is driving down the imaginary car park's spiral exit at speed.*

RIMMER: Speed bumps!

They bump up and down on their seats over three imaginary speed bumps.

RIMMER: Chicane!

They lean from side to side. Suddenly, RIMMER *looks through the 'windscreen' and reacts in horror.*

RIMMER: Look out – the barrier.

LISTER *'spots' it.*

LISTER: Brace yourselves – we're going through it!

They crash through the 'barrier' and skid on to the road. LISTER *wrestles the limo round with a nifty handbrake turn and guns off down the 'street'.*
   RIMMER *is looking out of the rear window.*

RIMMER: Motor cycles! Looks like they're carrying personal rocket launchers.
LISTER: (*Looking left*) That bridge. Think we can make it?
RIMMER: It's rising!
LISTER: Got any better ideas?

CAT: Do it!

LISTER *sweeps the car round and heads downhill towards the rising bridge. They hit the ramp on the bridge, and the car caroms into the air . . .*

ALL: Wooooooooooooaaaaaaaaaaaaahhhhhhhh!

HOLLY *shakes her head. They hit the other side of the bridge, bonnet down, straining the suspension to its limits.*

CAT: We made it. Nice driving. (*Salutes through the back window to the cops over the bridge.*) So long, suckers!
RIMMER: (*Looks up*) Uh-oh – helicopters.

Everyone looks at Rimmer, more than a bit pissed off.

LISTER: We're going to have to dump the limo.

He screeches into a side street, slams on the brakes and throws open the door.

LISTER: OK, come on! Go! Go, go, go!

They all leap out of the 'car', desperately looking around for cops and cover.

CAT: There! That alleyway.

They run round Starbug's rear section twice before dashing into the cockpit. We pick them up on the run in:

32. Pre-VT. Ext. Alley. Night
Very seedy and gloomy. Light comes from a flashing neon sign. Back in their alter ego costumes, LISTER, KRYTEN, RIMMER *and the* CAT *come to a halt, glancing nervously behind them for signs of the police. The* CAT *is clutching his wounded arm. In the distance, we hear a siren and, somewhere overhead, the sound of choppers.*

KRYTEN: I killed him. I killed a human.

116

Without any warning, KRYTEN *puts his gun to his temple and pulls the trigger. Click. It's empty. Click. Click. Click.*

KRYTEN: Damn!

KRYTEN *ejects the magazine and starts putting in a new one.*

LISTER: What are you doing?

KRYTEN: It is fundamental to me never to take a life. No matter what the provocation. I could have stunned him. I killed him. I must terminate myself.

KRYTEN *snaps in the new magazine.*

RIMMER: This is a nightmare! I'm on the run from the Fascist police with a murderer and a mass murderer and a man in a Bri-nylon shirt! I'm a piece of flotsam, jetsam, human-wreckage sputum bag, who smells like a yak latrine, and now my best flashing mac is about to get splattered with an android's brain. After you with the gun!

LISTER: Yeah, count me in, too.

CAT: Ditto.

KRYTEN: There's only one bullet left.

CAT: Well, we'll all put our heads together, and the bullet can go down the line.

They shuffle together, and arrange themselves so their ears are touching. And we cut back to:

33. Int. Starbug cockpit. Undersea

They are all lined up as in the alley, with KRYTEN *holding a vicious-looking harpoon gun to all of their heads.*

HOLLY: Kryten – I'm broadcasting on a higher frequency. Can you hear me now?

KRYTEN: Did somebody say something?

HOLLY: You're hallucinating! Put the gun down!

KRYTEN: I think I'm going to put the gun down.

He does so.

HOLLY: Walk forward three paces.

34. Pre-VT. Ext. Alley. Night

KRYTEN: I think I'm going to walk forward three paces.

KRYTEN *walks five paces to his right.*

RIMMER: *He's* cracking up.

KRYTEN: I feel a strange compulsion to pick up this fire extinguisher and twist the release wheel.

He picks up a battered old fire extinguisher and twists the wheel.

35. Int. Starbug cockpit. Undersea

KRYTEN *is holding the lithium carbonate canister, which is spewing gas from its nozzle.*

RIMMER: Have you quite finished being strange?

36. Pre-VT. Ext. Alley. Night

KRYTEN: Yes ... I ... I'm sorry – I don't know what overcame me.

He puts down the fire extinguisher, picks up the gun and stands at the end of the line.

KRYTEN: OK?

HOLLY: (*VO*) You're hallucinating.

37. Pre-VT. Ext. Alley. Night

HOLLY: You're hallucinating.

They all slowly turn and look at Holly.

LISTER: What?

HOLLY: I thought you weren't going to make it. Welcome back to reality.

LISTER: What happened?

HOLLY: You had a group hallucination, brought on by the ink from the despair squid. You were about to commit suicide, just like the crew of the *Esperanto*. Till the mood stabilizer saved you.

RIMMER: The lithium carbonate.

LISTER: We really would have killed ourselves?

KRYTEN: Of course — the hallucination was designed to induce despair: to attack the very things we each consider quintessential to our self esteem. Take Mr Rimmer. Back there he could no longer blame his failings and shortcomings on his parents because he shared his upbringing with you, sir: his richer, more important half-brother. The Cat lost his cool, and life for him no longer had any meaning, because he's so mind-meltingly shallow.

CAT: (*Flicks fingers*) Right! Superficial is my middle name.

KRYTEN: (*To Lister*) And you, sir. You have always prided yourself on being a good man, a man of moral courage, so when you thought you were a mass-murdering butcher for a totalitarian state — despair. Despair destined to drive you over the edge.

LISTER: And with you, it was taking a human life.

KRYTEN: Precisely.

CAT: I'm not Duane Dibbley?

KRYTEN: No.

RIMMER: I am Rimmer?

KRYTEN: I'm afraid so.

LISTER: What happened to the despair squid?

HOLLY: I took care of him: limpet mines. There's enough fried calamari out there to feed the whole of Italy.

CAT: Well, I say let's get out of here. Say old squidly-diddly back there has relatives, and Pop's out looking for him.

He's going to be mighty teed off when he finds Junior won't be going to this year's annual jellyfish ball.

38. Int. Starbug cockpit. Undersea

KRYTEN *and* LISTER *in the driving seats,* CAT *and* RIMMER *stand behind,* HOLLY *on monitor. They flick switches and make checks, preparing to launch from the ocean bed.*

HOLLY: Flight co-ordinates programmed, switching to pilot co-operation until we hit the surface.

LISTER: Those planet engineers screwed up in a big way here, didn't they? Playing God? The evolutionary process threw up a life form so much stronger and more deadly than any other species, it damned near wiped out everything on the entire planet, spreading despair and destruction wherever it stuck its ugly mush.

KRYTEN: Sounds rather reminiscent of a species sitting not a million miles away from me. (*Laughs. Stops – no one's joining in.*) You probably have to be a mechanoid to fully appreciate that one.

RIMMER: Kryten – no one likes a smart-alec android. Hit the retros.

KRYTEN: We're on our way, sir.

PSIRENS

1. Model shot
*Starfield. We pan to reveal enormous sun. After a pause, Starbug
beetles across the disc of the sun.*

2. Int. Obs. deck
*Dark. Various consoles click into life as we pan round the room,
and come to rest on two deep sleep units. Suddenly, one of them
flares with blue light from inside, and its hood hisses back, revealing
a slowly-waking, bearded* LISTER, *wearing soiled long johns. He
sits up. His mouth tastes vile. He notices his fingernails and
toenails are six inches long.* LISTER *pads across the room, and starts
to cut his nails in a desk-mounted pencil sharpener. He catches his
reflection in a blank TV screen.*

LISTER: (*To his reflection*) Who the hell are you?

3. Int. (OB) Starbug engine room
KRYTEN *empties some waste into a large hatch marked: 'Waste
Compactor' and presses the start button. Crushing sounds. He opens
the hatch and takes out the garbage, now in a perfect cube.*

4. Int. Mid-section
*More hi-tech than before. Light panels line the back wall. Switches,
radar screens, etc. There is a large flatbed scanner screen, which
doubles as a table, surrounded by four chairs.* KRYTEN *climbs up the*

spiral staircase with the waste cube. LISTER *is standing there, looking a bit nonplussed.*

KRYTEN: Welcome back on-line, sir. How are you feeling?

LISTER: I can't remember anything. I don't know who I am. What is this place? Who are you?

(*As he speaks,* KRYTEN *places the cube in a waste disposal chute and launches it into space.*)

KRYTEN: Ah, you have a touch of amnesia. That's quite common after such a long period in Deep Sleep. You've been out for just over two hundred years.

LISTER: Two hundred years?

KRYTEN: Actually, I woke you last spring, but you absolutely insisted on another three months.

LISTER: What did you say my name was?

KRYTEN: Lister, sir.

LISTER: And you are –?

LISTER *follows* KRYTEN *into:*

5. Int. Galley

KRYTEN: Lister. I was just preparing your breakfast tray.

LISTER *examines the tray.*

LISTER: These cornflakes have got grated raw onions sprinkled over them.

KRYTEN: That's how you like them, sir.

LISTER: Do I? (*Sips from glass. Winces.*) This orange juice is revolting.

KRYTEN: That's not orange juice, sir. That's your early-morning pick-me-up. Chilled vindaloo sauce.

LISTER: I drink cold curry sauce for breakfast?

KRYTEN: Depends on your mood. If you get up in the afternoon, you often prefer to start the day with a can of last night's flat lager. That's why you sleep with a tea strainer by your bed: to sieve out the cigar dimps.

LISTER: I drink, I smoke, I have curry sauce for breakfast? Raw onions on my cereal? I sound like some barely human grossed-out slime ball.

KRYTEN: Oh excellent, sir. It's all flooding back then?

LISTER: No. None of it is.

KRYTEN *sets a box in front of Lister.*

KRYTEN: Perhaps these will help. Your personal artefacts. You asked me to keep them safe.

LISTER *takes out a photo.*

KRYTEN: Kristine Kochanski. You dated her for three weeks once. Before she discarded you for a catering officer.

LISTER: She's beautiful.

KRYTEN: It's your ambition, sir, some day, somehow to get her back and lie on top of her and move up and down rapidly in that curious way that humans find so agreeable. Personally, I prefer partnership whist.

LISTER *takes out a book.*

LISTER: Ah! Wait a minute. This feels more like it. Aristotle's *Metaphysica*. At last – something wholesome and commend-able about me.

KRYTEN: Hardly, sir. You use that book to hide your secret Polaroid collection of naked ex-girlfriends.

LISTER: (*Looking through them*) God, I went out with a lot of nurses, didn't I?

KRYTEN: I don't believe those are authentic uniforms, sir. Note the astonishing brevity of those hemlines. I believe *all* those girls are impostors, pretending to belong to the medical profession for some nefarious purpose as yet un-known.

KRYTEN *hands* LISTER *his guitar.*

LISTER: Is this mine? Do I play the guitar?

KRYTEN: Do you play the guitar? Do I have a head shaped like an amusing ice cube? Why don't you chock out a few power chords? See if anything comes back to you.

LISTER *plucks tunelessly at the strings.*

KRYTEN: The Axeman's back!

LISTER: Don't patronize me. I can't play the guitar. Anyone with half an ear can tell that.

KRYTEN: Please, sir — you are not yourself at present. When you're fully functional, and your personality's restored, you will firmly believe you can play the guitar like the ghost of Hendrix.

LISTER: Is there something good you can tell me about myself? Something laudable?

KRYTEN: Laudable ... Well, you frequently help me with my laundry duties by wearing your underpants inside out and extending their wear time by three weeks.

LISTER: I'm an animal! I'm a tasteless, uncouth, tone-deaf, mindless, revolting, randy, blokeish, semi-literate space bum.

KRYTEN: (*Gives him a bear hug.*) Welcome back, Davey!

KRYTEN *opens the fridge, gets out Rimmer's frozen light bee and pops it into a pan of boiling water.*

LISTER: What's that?

KRYTEN: Mr Rimmer, sir. He's a hologram, sir. This is his light bee.

LISTER: Rimmer ... He's my best mate, isn't he?

KRYTEN: You *are* sick, sir. I'm getting worried. Maybe a little synaptic enhancer will do the trick.

KRYTEN *takes out syringe gun and fires it into Lister's neck.*

KRYTEN *takes the light bee out of the water and places it in an egg cup. And* LISTER *follows* KRYTEN *into:*

6. Int. Mid-section

KRYTEN *places the light bee on the scanner and sits in front of the computer screen on the rear wall.*

KRYTEN: Initiating boot-up sequence.

KRYTEN *taps some panels on the keyboard, and the light bee flares into life and hovers out of the egg cup.*

KRYTEN: Download physical form.

Rimmer's image crackles into existence around the light bee, in black and white, with ripples of white noise interference.

KRYTEN: Access personality banks.

On the screen: a bar chart appears.

KRYTEN: Download characteristics. Load arrogance.

The first bar (a tall one) shrinks towards the bottom of the screen, like liquid being poured from a vial, to the accompaniment of appropriate computer sound effects.

KRYTEN: Load charisma.

The second bar (a very, very short one) disappears off screen with a single blip!

KRYTEN: Load neuroses.

The next, the longest bar, drains off the screen. Followed by the next, and the next, and the next . . . RIMMER *becomes fully formed and colourful.*

KRYTEN: Download memory.

As RIMMER *receives his memory, his face contorts into various combinations of horror, shock, anguish, and occasional brief spasms of joy. He gets his bearings.*

LISTER: Oh. *That* Rimmer.

7. Int. Mid-section
They are all sitting around the scanner scope. The CAT is cracking the head of a boiled mouse in an egg cup. RIMMER is looking at him aghast. LISTER is tucking into his cornflakes.

LISTER: Good cornflakes. Nice and oniony. Pass me the Tabasco sauce – just needs a bit more pep in it.

KRYTEN: Congratulations, sir. You seem to be on your way to full recall. Next thing you know, you'll be convinced you can play the guitar.

LISTER: (*Astonished*) I can play the guitar! I'm a diva, man. I can make that lump of wood sing like a Yukon bear trapper on his annual visit to the brothel.

CAT: That's as maybe, bud. But the deal stays the same.

LISTER: I know, I know. If I want to strum my guitar, I have to put on a suit and do it in outer space. Peasants.

LISTER *liberally douses the cornflakes with Tabasco, then swigs from the bottle.*

KRYTEN: Suggest we begin debriefing. Mr Rimmer?

RIMMER: Thank you, Kryten. Gentlemen, as we're all aware, we have lost Red Dwarf. This is not the time for small-minded, petty recrimination. The time for that is when Lister is court-martialled after we get back to Earth.

LISTER: I didn't lose it.

RIMMER: You're the one who parked it, Lister. You're the one who couldn't remember which planetoid you'd left it around.

LISTER: Yeah, but they all look the same, those little blue-green planetoids. They're all sort of little, blue-green and planetoidy.

KRYTEN: Sirs, please, there's no advantage in finger-pointing. We didn't lose Red Dwarf. Red Dwarf was stolen. By persons . . . or life forms unknown.

CAT: Who would steal a gigantic red trash can with no brakes and three million years on the clock?

KRYTEN: Rogue droids . . . Genetically engineered life forms . . . Figments of Mr Lister's imagination made solid by some weird space ray. Who knows? The important thing is, after two hundred years of following their vapour trail, we have them.

LISTER: What d'you mean?

KRYTEN *clears some breakfast things off the scanner screen.*

KRYTEN: They've been forced to make a massive detour to circumnavigate this asteroid belt. However, *Starbug* is small enough to negotiate its way directly through the middle. For the first time in two centuries, we have the opportunity to head them off at the pass, as it were, and recover Holly.

CAT: Well, what are we waiting for?

RIMMER: Without deflectors? What about Space Corps Directive one-seven-four-two?

KRYTEN: One-seven-four-two? 'No member of the Corps should ever report for active duty in a ginger toupee'? Thanks for reminding us of that regulation, sir. But is it really that pertinent in this particular situation?

RIMMER: One-seven-four-*three*, then.

KRYTEN: Oh, I *see*. 'No registered vessel should attempt to transverse an asteroid belt without deflectors.'

RIMMER: Yes? God, he's pedantic.

LISTER: Rimmer, check out the supply situation. (*Indicates computer printout.*) Your hologram's on battery back-up. We've only got oxygen for three months: water, if we drink re-cyc, seven weeks. And worst of all, we're down to our last two thousand poppadoms. We're in trouble, big time.

RIMMER: You know how unstable these belts are. Rogue asteroids ... meteor storms. One direct hit on that plexiglass viewscreen, and our innards will be turned inside out quicker than a pair of Lister's old underpants.

LISTER: We're out of options, man. We're taking her in.

KRYTEN: Recommend the Cat pilots. His superior reflexes and nasal intuition will give us our best chance.

CAT, LISTER *and* KRYTEN *stand to leave.*

RIMMER: For pity's sake, one breech in that hull, and we're people paté.

CAT: There's an old Cat proverb: 'It's better to live one hour as a tiger, than a whole lifetime as a worm.'

RIMMER: There's an old human saying: 'Whoever heard of a wormskin rug?'

8. Model shot

Starbug's *rear jets flare and it arcs into the asteroid belt.*

9. Model shot

We see the back of Starbug *as it tacks through a narrow gap between two huge asteroids.*

10. Int. Cockpit

All at their stations. Tense. Suddenly, orange light flares from their right. CAT *wrenches the controls to the left.*

11. Model shot

A huge lick of flame leaps out at Starbug *from a gas geyser on one of the asteroids.*

12. Int. Cockpit

Starbug *nicks the opposite asteroid as it swerves to avoid the flame, and they all stagger with the impact.*

LISTER: Nice stick work, man.

CAT *wrinkles his nose.*

CAT: Something's coming.

KRYTEN: Nothing on the navicomp.

CAT: I can smell it. (*Peers through screen.*) Something big.

LISTER: I'm getting nothing, either.

CAT: These nostrils never lie.

RIMMER: He's right. Co-ordinates 1746 by 9472. Take a peek, gentlemen. There's a meteor bigger than King Kong's first dump of the day, and it's screaming straight towards us.

KRYTEN: It's far too vast to go around.

RIMMER: Reverse thrust.

CAT: There's no time. Face it – we're deader than corduroy.

LISTER: Kryten, you know what to do.

KRYTEN: On my way, sir.

RIMMER: Lister. Given that we've got as much chance of getting out of this in one piece as a Jammy Dodger that's been dunked in hot coffee and wiggled about for three minutes, perhaps you'd do me the courtesy of explaining what he's doing?

LISTER: He souped up the waste disposal. Filled the eject system with rocket fuel, and turned it into a sort of high-impact garbage cannon.

RIMMER: A garbage cannon? You're going to try and shoot that out of the sky with tin cans and banana peel?

LISTER: There's a thermos of nitro-glycerine in there, too.

KRYTEN *picks up a cube of garbage, opens a hatch in the wall marked 'Waste disposal unit 5' and places the cube in the chute inside.*

KRYTEN: Waste disposal unit armed, and ready to fire.

RIMMER: Kryten – will this work?

KRYTEN: Lie Mode. (*Pause.*) Of course it will work, sir. No worries. (*Winks to Lister*) Hook, line, sinker, rod and copy of *Angling Times.*

CAT: Here it comes!

LISTER: Bearing zero-seven-niner-two. Fire!

KRYTEN *pulls the waste disposal lever.*

13. Model shot

The waste cube blasts out of an orifice above Starbug's front lights, heads straight for the giant meteor, hits it in the middle and blasts it to pieces.

14. Int. Cockpit

ALL *whoop and cheer, apart from* RIMMER *who shakes his head in disbelief.*

KRYTEN: Relocating Red Dwarf's vapour trail. Present speed and course, estimated time of interception, twelve hours, seven minutes.

CAT: (*Sniffs.*) Check out your screens. I'm getting something new, and it does not smell good.

RIMMER: Enhance four. Nothing. Enhance eight . . . Sixteen. (*Shakes head.*) Thirty-two . . . Still nix. Enhance sixty-four. Got it. Some kind of ship.

LISTER: Wait a minute. There's another one. And another.

KRYTEN: I'm getting them too. Ten of them . . . twelve.

RIMMER: All derelict.

LISTER: It looks like this is some kind of spaceship graveyard.

15. Model shot

A tiny Starbug flies between a group of asteroids, all with wrecked space craft embedded in them.

16. Int. Cockpit

LISTER: Anyone else get the feeling that we've been led here like lambs to the kebab shop?

RIMMER: We are not moving another inch until we've found out what brought these ships down.

KRYTEN: Recommend we stop engines and launch scouter.

CAT *flicks some switches.*

CAT: Engines stopped. Launching scouter.

Sound effects: scouter launched. Cut to:

17. OB. Int. Crashed ship

We are inside. A laser burns a circle in the hull, which falls inwards, and scouter's search beam pierces the smoke as it hovers through the hole into the ship.

18. Int. Mid-section

LISTER, RIMMER, KRYTEN *and the* CAT *hunched over the scanner screen.*

KRYTEN: We're in.

19. OB. Int. Crashed ship

Scouter's POV now, as it hovers its way through the derelict craft. Dark and scary.

20. Int. Mid-section

LISTER: Scouter, stop. Go back. Stop. Angle, forty-five degrees to your left. Magnify.

CAT: What's that?

RIMMER: Human remains. Wait. Angle: five degrees right. Ten degrees up. Stop. There: some kind of writing on the floor. P-S-I-R-E-N-S. Psirens?

KRYTEN: The poor devil scrawled it in his death throes, using a combination of his own blood and even some lengths of his own intestines.

RIMMER: Who would do that?

LISTER: Someone who badly needed a pen.

CAT: What I don't understand is why he went to the trouble of using his kidney as a full stop.

RIMMER: I don't think he meant that. It probably just plopped out.

KRYTEN: Whoever he was, clearly he was desperate to warn any poor wretches who wandered into the same deadly trap.

They exchange worried looks.

LISTER: Scouter's located the black box. Replay final entry.

On the screen: white noise, which settles to become . . .

21. OB. Int. Crashed ship

All on one shot, overhead, wide-angle. Mad ASTRO, *wide-eyed with fear, talks directly to the camera eating a burger ravenously.*

ASTRO: They're closing in. They're all over the ship. They've got Hank, and Ludo. Tina, Jerry, Tim, Gordy, Sam. They even got Jeff. At least I think so: I found a huge pile of his intestines on his bunk. Maybe the rest of him escaped, I don't know. What am I saying? I'm half-crazed with fear. I know I'm next. It's just a matter of time before . . .

From the doorway behind him, a hideous INSECTOID *biped with mandibles advances towards him.*

INSECTOID: (*Speaks disgusting, incomprehensible insect language.*)

ASTRO: Oh God, you're so beautiful, I can't resist you. But I have to be strong. I know what you want.

INSECTOID: (*Insect talk.*)

ASTRO: No, you don't. You want to love me. You want to suck out my brains with a straw, like you did the rest of them.

INSECTOID: (*Insect talk.*)

ASTRO: I'm different? Is that what you said to Jeff? Just before you slurped up the contents of his skull, like it was a double-thick brain shake? Get away from me.

The INSECTOID *reaches him. He backs out of shot, the creature holds up a metal straw and follows. The* ASTRO *screams. The screen is splattered with red.*

ASTRO: (*VO*) What have you done, you evil harlot! You've squeezed all the ketchup out of my burger. Now what! No! Get that straw out of my ear!

There is a slurping sound and more gunk hits the screen. The INSECTOID *lurches into view, something grey and slimy dangling from its mouth. It sucks it in like spaghetti, then licks the screen.*

22. Int. Mid-section
The four of them watching the replay on the scanner screen. Without changing expression, RIMMER *falls backwards out of shot in a dead faint.*

23. Model shot
Starbug gingerly tacks through the spaceship graveyard.

24. Int. Mid-section
All seated round the scanner table. LISTER *has a sheaf of papers.*

LISTER: OK. Scouter's checked out black boxes on three of the derelicts. This entire belt is swarming with some kind of genetically engineered life form who can alter your perception, telepathically. They're called Psirens. Like with Ulysses in the ancient Turkish legend.

KRYTEN: I believe the legend was Greek, sir.

LISTER: Whatever. Some country that's big on curly shoes

and hoummos. The point is, they use this power of illusion to lure you on to the asteroids, strip the ships of anything they can use and suck out your brains.

RIMMER: They shouldn't bother us, then. There's barely a snack on board.

KRYTEN: We can't turn back. We'll lose Red Dwarf.

LISTER: Look, we'll be through the belt in three, maybe four hours. We've just got to be on our toes. They'll try and tempt us, scare us, break our morale – anything to force us down on to the rocks. Just be alert.

A wall monitor starts to fizzle with white noise.

CAT: Incoming message. It's pretty weak.

CAT *crosses to the monitor and fine-tunes the controls. The screen clears, and*

25. Int. Cushiony, curtainy area

Two beautiful TEMPTRESSES *appear.*

TEMPTRESS 1: Please help us. Our settlement is almost extinct. There are only women left.

TEMPTRESS 2: Barely three thousand of us.

TEMPTRESS 1: If we are to survive, we need males to spread their seed among our number. We beg you. Make love to us.

TEMPTRESS 2: Make love to all of us. Please, we beseech you . . .

26. Int. Mid-section

The screen dies.

CAT: You heard 'em – they want seed-spreaders. I'm going to apply. You guys deal with the Psiren thing. I'll deal with this.

CAT *dashes into the cockpit. Pause. He steps back again.*

CAT: Call me paranoid, but you don't think they were these Psiren dude things . . .?

LISTER, RIMMER *and* KRYTEN *nod patiently.*

CAT: Even the brunette?

LISTER, RIMMER *and* KRYTEN *nod.*

CAT: You don't think there's any chance they're just two nice girls who both happen to want my seed for totally legitimate reasons?

LISTER, RIMMER *and* KRYTEN *shake their heads.*

CAT: I don't need to tell you this is a big disappointment. Damn vixens! How could they be so cunning? If anyone wants me, I'll be taking a cold shower in liquid oxygen.

CAT *exits to cockpit.*

RIMMER: Well, if that's the most sophisticated enticement these Psirens can throw at us, I hardly think we're exactly in danger of being bewitched.

KRYTEN: If I may postulate, sir: that was merely the level of sophistication required to lure the Cat. And it worked. Had we not stopped him, he would now be on one of those asteroids, crawling around without his brain, trying to write 'Oh boy, was *I* suckered' with his own intestinal tract.

LISTER: Look, we'll make it. All we've got to do is stay on the case.

The screen fizzles.

LISTER: Incoming message. Here they come again.

The picture is riddled with interference.

27. Int. Ship interior

A wounded WOMAN *looks into camera. In the background, through the smoke, we can vaguely make out that the* WOMAN *and her companions are fighting a futile rearguard action. She is talking into a communicator.*

WOMAN: Can anyone read me? This is Captain Tau of the SCS *Pioneer*. We're under attack from some kind of scavengers – Psirens. They lured us on to this god-forsaken asteroid – killed most of the crew.

She turns and lets out a volley of laser fire.

LISTER: Is this genuine?

The WOMAN *is shot dead. A second* WOMAN *picks up the communicator, and turns to the screen.*

KOCHANSKI: Don't try and help us. We're finished. Save yourselves.

LISTER: Kochanski!

KOCHANSKI: Dave? Is that you?

LISTER: I thought you were dead.

KOCHANSKI: No time to explain. We're over-run! Get out of the belt while you can!

LISTER: It's Kochanski.

KOCHANSKI: We'll be OK – they'll never take us alive. I'm keeping back three bullets. One for me and one each for the two kids.

LISTER: Kids?

KOCHANSKI: Your two sons, Dave.

LISTER: My sons? But how . . .? I don't understand.

KOCHANSKI: When you went into stasis, I broke into the sperm bank, Dave, back on Red Dwarf. You're a father. (*Turns.*) Here they come! (*Cocks gun and calls off.*) Jim, Bexley, come to Mummy.

LISTER: Wait! Don't do anything. I'm coming in.

The screen blanks.

28. Int. Mid-section

LISTER: Kryten – get the bazookoids. Rimmer – plot a course.

LISTER *grabs a space helmet.*

RIMMER: Lister – tune into Sanity FM.
LISTER: What? Are you saying they were . . . Psirens?
RIMMER: Of course. It's as plain as a Bulgarian pin-up.
LISTER: You're sure?
RIMMER: Come on, Listy, you're giving simpletons a bad name.

CAT *leans in from cockpit.*

CAT: I think you should take a look at this. Something's heading straight for us.
KRYTEN: What is it?
CAT: What do you call one of those giant meteorites that are covered in flames?
KRYTEN: A giant, flaming meteorite?
CAT: That's it!

29. Model shot
Flaming meteor hurtling through space.

30. Int. Cockpit
All take up their stations.

KRYTEN: Should I load the garbage cannon?
LISTER: Wouldn't make a dent.
RIMMER: Plot course change.

KRYTEN *turns to navicomp.*

CAT: Engaging re-heat!

KRYTEN: Wait! There's nothing on the radar.

RIMMER: So?

KRYTEN: I think it's another illusion.

LISTER: Psirens?

KRYTEN: Cat? Are you getting any scent from that meteorite?

CAT: Scent? You think there's going to be a duty-free shop on it?

KRYTEN: Can you *smell* anything?

CAT: No. (*Looks at* RIMMER.) Just a little holo-fear.

KRYTEN: Recommend we maintain current course. That fireball does not exist.

RIMMER: Say you're wrong?

KRYTEN: Sir, I'll stake my reputation on it.

RIMMER: Kryten, you haven't got a reputation.

KRYTEN: No, but I hope to acquire one from this escapade.

LISTER: It's closing. Too late to run.

The others brace themselves. KRYTEN *remains defiantly erect.*

KRYTEN: Relax, gentlemen, we're quite safe.

31. Model shot
The flaming meteor hurtles towards Starbug ... and passes harmlessly through it.

32. Int. Cockpit
They are momentarily bathed in an orange glow, then back to normal. They unbrace.

KRYTEN: Well, I can't hang around saving your necks all day. Swagger mode.

KRYTEN *swaggers out.*

KRYTEN: Guess I'd better make a start on that ironing.

LISTER *follows him.*

CAT: (*Sniffs the air.*) I'm getting another one. (*To* RIMMER.) Better get Kryten. He'll tell us what to do.

RIMMER: I'm perfectly capable of dealing with a giant, flaming meteorite, thank you so very much. We do not need to enlist the help of a domestic droid with a head shaped like a genetically flawed lumpfish.

CAT: OK, keep your H on. So what do we do?

RIMMER: There's nothing on the radar. It's another illusion. We do nothing.

LISTER *and* KRYTEN *come back in.*

LISTER: What's happening, guys? Cabin temperature's rising.

RIMMER: Psirens again. Another illusion. It's all in hand.

KRYTEN: Permission to speak, sir?

RIMMER: Refused.

KRYTEN: What if this time it's a real fireball and the radar read-out that's the illusion?

RIMMER: Relax, gentlemen. We're quite safe.

LISTER: Cat – chuck a left, man.

They brace themselves, except for RIMMER, *who stands nobly erect.*

33. Model shot
The flaming meteor hurtles towards Starbug . . . *and smashes into it.*

34. Int. Cockpit
RIMMER *gets flung backwards through the cockpit door. Sparks and smoke from the consoles.*

35. Model shot. Night
Starbug *crashes on to an asteroid.*

36. Int. Cockpit

LISTER *and* CAT *are putting out small fires on the consoles.*
KRYTEN *is checking the computer screen.* RIMMER *staggers in.*

RIMMER: Any damage?

CAT: Not too bad. A couple of the sensors are out, fuel-intake chambers are both flooded and the left pilot seat doesn't go up and down any more.

RIMMER: We came through that intact?

KRYTEN: *Starbug* was built to last, sir. This old baby's crashed more times than a ZX81.

LISTER: It's the material it's built from. Aerospace engineers discovered that, after a plane crash, the only thing that always survives intact is a cute little doll. They built *Starbug* out of the same stuff.

CAT: How long before we can take off again?

KRYTEN: Oh, just a matter of . . . Wait. The front landing stanchion is embedded in the rock up to its joint. We're going to have to go out there and blast it free.

LISTER: I'll go.

KRYTEN: Sir, the atmosphere is thin, and this place is likely to be crawling with Psirens.

LISTER: You sort out the engines. I'll be out there two minutes, maximum.

37. Model shot. Night

Crashed Starbug. *Tiny sparks by the front landing leg. We cut to:*

38. Ext. (OB) Asteroid. Night

Welding gun held by LISTER, *in space suit, as he tries to free* Starbug*'s landing leg. Attached to the neck of the suit is a breathing pipe, which looks a bit like a harmonica, from which he occasionally sucks air. He stops and presses a communicator button on his wrist.*

LISTER: How's that?

CAT: (*VO. Dist.*). Looking good. We'll clear the rest on take-off.

LISTER: On my way back.

LISTER *packs his gear. From behind him, he hears:*

PSIREN: Hi, Dave.

LISTER *spins to see a* PSIREN — *a cross between Catwoman and Barbarella.*

LISTER: Smegging heck. It's Pete Tranter's sister!

PETE TRANTER'S SISTER: Remember me, Dave? You lusted after me all through your puberty. There's nothing more potent than an adolescent fantasy. Don't you remember? You wanted me so badly: you even made a special hole in your pocket. And now, at last, I can be yours.

LISTER *trains his welding gun on her.*

LISTER: Back off, Pete Tranter's sister! I know what you're after: it's moist and pink and it's inside my head. And that's where it's staying.

PETE TRANTER'S SISTER: Oh, come on, Dave. You know what you want. You want to squeeze my buttocks together to make one juicy giant peach.

LISTER: I get it. You're trying to make me drown in my own drool. Well, it won't work.

PETE TRANTER'S SISTER: Don't fight it.

PETE TRANTER'S SISTER *advances. On the ground we see the shadow she casts is her true form: the hideous bipedal insectoid we saw before.* LISTER, *unaware, swoons and sways, trying to fight his desire.*

LISTER: Stay back, Pete Tranter's sister.

PETE TRANTER'S SISTER: How long has it been since you made love to a woman?

LISTER: I admit it's been a while.

PETE TRANTER'S SISTER: It's been over three million years, Dave.

LISTER: I prefer to count it in Ice Ages; then it's just four. And if you count it in *leap* Ice Ages, it's hardly even one.

PETE TRANTER'S SISTER: That's a long time, Dave, for a man of your drives.

LISTER: That's a long time for a Welsh shepherd who's allergic to wool.

PETE TRANTER'S SISTER: Kiss me.

Two-shot: as the PSIREN *approaches* LISTER, *we see it in its insectoid form.*

LISTER: I can't resist you any more, Pete Tranter's sister.

PETE TRANTER'S SISTER: Your death will be exquisite. I'll take you to the peak of ecstasy, then I'll blow your mind.

We intercut between LISTER *passionately necking with* PETE TRANTER'S SISTER *and* LISTER *necking with the hideous* INSECTOID PSIREN, *including licking its swarfega-dripping mandibles. Slowly,* PETE TRANTER'S SISTER *raises a metal straw, like we saw in the mad Astro scene, about to plunge it into his head, when a shot rings out and* PETE TRANTER'S SISTER *is hit in the back. Before Lister's eyes, the illusion ends and he sees the* INSECTOID PSIREN *thrashing around on the ground, squealing in its death throes. He looks up.* KRYTEN *holds a smoking bazookoid.*

KRYTEN: Come on, Dave – let's get out of here.

As LISTER *walks past him, we see* KRYTEN *is concealing a metal straw behind his back.*

LISTER: (*To himself.*) Dave??

Slo-mo: LISTER *spins as the metal straw arcs down towards his head. He blasts* KRYTEN. *The illusion ends and another* INSECTOID PSIREN *dies, jerking and squealing. Lister's radio crackles.*

KRYTEN: (*VO. Dist.*) Sir? Is everything OK out there?

LISTER: Stand by with the airlock. I'm coming back.

39. Int. Cockpit

RIMMER *and* KRYTEN *craning over the mike.*

RIMMER: What's the delay?

LISTER: (*VO. Dist.*) A couple of Psirens wiped each other out fighting over my brains ... Oh, no. It's the TV weather girl from Channel 27.

KRYTEN: Sir. Fight it! Don't look at her.

LISTER: (*VO. Dist.*) It's not that easy, Kryten – you can't see what she's doing with her pointy stick.

CAT: I'm starting up the engines.

RIMMER: Get back in here.

KRYTEN *exits to mid-section. Over the radio, we hear Lister firing.*

LISTER: (*VO. Dist.*) On my way.

CAT *starts up the engines.*

40. Int. Mid-section

KRYTEN *stands by the airlock, looking at a video monitor. The monitor blinks into life and* LISTER *appears.*

LISTER: (*VO. Dist.*) It's me.

KRYTEN *presses a button.*

41. Int. (OB). Airlock doors

The outer airlock doors hiss open (A flat), and through swirling smoke, LISTER *steps in. He presses the door close button.*

LISTER: I'm in.

42. Int. Mid-section

KRYTEN *opens the inner airlock and closes it as* LISTER *staggers in.*

LISTER: It's getting pretty hairy out there. Come on — let's vamoose.

43. Int. Cockpit

CAT *starts to take off.*

44. Int. Mid-section

As KRYTEN *and* LISTER *head for the cockpit, the airlock monitor fizzes on again and a* SECOND LISTER *appears on the screen.*

LISTER 2: What the hell are you doing taking off when I'm still outside? Let me in.

KRYTEN *double-takes between the* LISTER *inside and the* LISTER *on the monitor.*

KRYTEN: I'm afraid, sir, you're already here.

RIMMER *steps down from cockpit.*

LISTER 1: He's a Psiren. Don't let him in.

LISTER 2: For god's sake — I can't hang on any longer. *He's* the Psiren. Let me in!

RIMMER· What do we do?

KRYTEN There's no way to tell which is which. We have to let him in

RIMMER: That means we'll definitely have a Psiren on board. A brain-sucking psychotic temporal lobe slurper.

KRYTEN: There's a fifty per cent chance we have one on board already. We can't risk killing the real Lister. I'm letting him in.

RIMMER: What about Space Corps directive 5796?

KRYTEN: 5796? 'No officer above the rank of mess sergeant is permitted to go into combat with pierced nipples'?!? Pardon me, but how does that possibly pertain to the current situation?

RIMMER: 5797, then.

KRYTEN: The hell with the regs, sir. I'm letting him in.

KRYTEN *presses the door release.*

RIMMER: On your square head be it.

45. Model shot
Starbug *flying through asteroid belt.*

46. Int. Mid-section
The TWO LISTERS *are seated side by side,* KRYTEN *has a bazookoid trained on them.* RIMMER *watches them warily. The* CAT *steps down from the cockpit and picks up a bazookoid.*

CAT: We're on auto.

LISTER 1: How many times? *He's* the Psiren, I'm me.

LISTER 2: How can you believe this for two seconds? He doesn't even *look* like me. He's podgy. He hasn't got my classic profile.

KRYTEN: Sir, you both look identical.

The TWO LISTERS *look at each other, then look forward.*

LISTER 1 *and* 2: (*Together.*) No way.

KRYTEN: We're going to try some tests.

RIMMER: A series of questions to trick and confuse you. If you fail to answer correctly or for any reason hesitate, you'll be shot.

LISTER 1: Come on, Rimmer, give us a break.

LISTER 2: (*Overlapping.*) For god's sake, Rimmer, do me a lemon.

RIMMER: Kryten?

KRYTEN *throws two apples.* BOTH LISTERS *catch them right-handed.*

RIMMER: Both right-handed. Correct. You have a tattoo on your left buttock, true or false?

LISTER 1 and 2: (*Together*) True.

RIMMER: (*To* LISTER 1) You. It's dedicated to the one unbending love of your life. Describe the tattoo.

LISTER 1: It's a heart with an arrow through it, and underneath it says 'I love vindaloo' in dripping curry sauce.

RIMMER: (*To* LISTER 2) You. How did you get it?

LISTER 2: Planet leave on Ganymede. Went on the razz with Petersen. He spiked my cocktail with half a pint of four star petrol. When I next awoke, I'd enrolled as a novice monk in a Ganymedian monastery. I discovered the vindaloo tattoo when I handed in my habit.

RIMMER: Take your shoes and socks off. Kryten?

KRYTEN *puts two pairs of scissors on the scanner top.*

RIMMER: Now, gentlemen: trim your toe nails.

Both LISTERS *start biting their toenails.*

RIMMER: Enough.

KRYTEN *picks up Lister's guitar and hands it to* LISTER 1.

RIMMER: Play the guitar.

LISTER 1: Here? Inside?

RIMMER: Play it.

LISTER 1 *starts playing the guitar. It is a superb display of axemanship. (If we could get some guitar diva to crouch behind Lister and be his arms, ecstasy.) After about fifteen seconds of astonishing virtuosity, the music builds to a crescendo and ends. As the last chord dies away,* KRYTEN *and the* CAT *hit* LISTER 1 *with volley after volley of bazookoid fire. The* INSECTOID PSIREN *writhes and screeches on the floor.*

LISTER 2: How did you know that wasn't me?

CAT: 'Cause that dude could play.

LISTER 2: He wasn't any better than me.

KRYTEN: That's how you *believe* you play, sir. That's why, when the Psiren read your mind, he shared your delusion that you are not a ten-thumbed, tone-deaf, talentless noise polluter.

LISTER: Are you seriously saying you think he was better than me?

LISTER *picks up the guitar and starts playing. It's terrible.*

LISTER: What's the difference? If anything, this is slightly better.

CAT: A little survival tip, bud. Never play your guitar in front of a man with a loaded gun.

LISTER: I resent this. I resent you saving my life in this way. I won't forget this.

RIMMER: Where's it gone?

ALL *look down for the Psiren's corpse. It has vanished. A trail of yellow Psiren blood leads to the spiral staircase.*

KRYTEN: It's crawled down to the engine room.

Alert lights flash and a siren whoops.

RIMMER: Meteor storm! Off the port bow. It's a biggie.

KRYTEN: Recommend you two stay and man the cockpit. Mr Rimmer and I will pursue the Psiren.

RIMMER: Um, that's quite a good plan, Kryten. Excellent in all but one detail. I think you know what it is. (*Waves.*) 'Bye.

KRYTEN: There's no time to argue.

KRYTEN *heads for the spiral stairs. The others dash into the cockpit. After a short pause, the bloodstain trail vanishes, and the wounded* PSIREN *drops its illusion of invisibility and re-appears where it fell.*

47. Int. (OB) Engine room

KRYTEN *prowls around with his psi-scan and bazookoid. He gets an alert beep on his psi-scan, and rotates. He looks up. The wounded* PSIREN *is behind him, some distance away.*

KRYTEN: Please. I have no desire to hurt you. Let us set you down on an asteroid where your fellow GELFs can attend to your wounds.

The PSIREN *rasps insectly.*

KRYTEN: There's no logic in trying to engage me in combat. I am unseducible, in that I have no desires or lusts, and my brain is synthetic and consequently of no interest to you. Give yourself up.

KRYTEN *looks astonished. When we cut back, the* PSIREN *has become a female scientist,* MAMET.

KRYTEN: Professor Mamet? My creator.
MAMET: Hello, Kryten.
KRYTEN: What is the function of this illusion?

MAMET *starts to advance on him.*

MAMET: You cannot harm me, Kryten. It's coded into every cell in your body. You're totally defenceless against me.

KRYTEN *lowers his bazookoid and takes out his walkie-talkie.*

KRYTEN: True. However, the others are not so hampered.
MAMET: You are also programmed to obey my every command. Drop the radio.

KRYTEN *involuntarily drops the walkie-talkie.*

MAMET: Open the waste compactor.

Against his will, KRYTEN *opens the waste compactor we saw earlier.*

KRYTEN: What are you doing?
MAMET: Climb inside.
KRYTEN: No!

But he climbs inside.

KRYTEN: This serves no . . .
MAMET: Engage the mechanism.
KRYTEN: You're sick!

KRYTEN *struggles with himself but loses. He presses the compactor button. The hatch closes.*

MAMET: Die!

We hear the sound of Kryten being crushed. A silence. We hear footsteps on the metal stairs. MAMET *wheels round. Shot:* LISTER, *the* CAT *and* RIMMER *walking along the gantry.*

LISTER: Kryten? You here? The meteor storm was another illusion. The Psiren's not as badly wounded as we thought.
RIMMER: Kryten?

They spot Kryten's psi-scan and bazookoid, abandoned on the floor.

CAT: It's got him.

LISTER *picks up the psi-scan and activates it.*

LISTER: (*Shouts*) Kryten?

48. Int. (OB) Another section of engine room

CAT, LISTER *and* RIMMER *walk down some stairs.* RIMMER *suddenly fades to black and white.*

RIMMER: My battery's going. Only a few seconds left. Need a recharge . . .

Rimmer's image vanishes, and his light bee falls to the floor. LISTER *picks it up and pockets it.*

LISTER: Then there were two.

CAT and LISTER round a corner. We see the INSECTOID PSIREN standing against a wall. Bizarrely, CAT and LISTER don't react but walk straight up to it.

LISTER: (*To* CAT) Want a drink, man?
CAT: I'm parched.

LISTER stands facing the PSIREN.

LISTER: (*To* CAT) Cola?

From another angle, we see what they see: a Coke machine. LISTER reaches for a button.

LISTER: Wait a minute. What's a vending machine doing in the engine room?

In a flurry of arms, mandibles and prosboces, the INSECTOID PSIREN attacks CAT and LISTER, knocking them both out. As they lie helpless, the INSECTOID PSIREN takes out the metal straw. They are dead meat.

49. Int. (OB) Engine room
The waste compactor hatch springs open, and KRYTEN drops out. He has been compacted into a cube, with short, stumpy legs but no arms.

KRYTEN: You scum-sucking mollusc. You can't do this to us.

He waddles furiously down the corridor. He catches sight of them on the deck below.

50. Int. (OB) Another section of engine room
The INSECTOID has the woozy LISTER by the locks, about to plunge the straw into his brain. We see CUBED KRYTEN plummet down towards the INSECTOID. The INSECTOID looks up, but too late, as CUBED KRYTEN crushes it.

51. Model shot. Starbug in Space

52. Int. Cockpit
CAT *in pilot seat,* LISTER *next to him.* RIMMER *at navicomp.*

RIMMER: That's it — we're clear of the belt.

LISTER: What about Red Dwarf?

RIMMER: According to the navicomp, it's gone into that gas nebula.

CAT: Then that's where we're heading.

The CUBED KRYTEN *waddles in with a tea tray on top of him.*

KRYTEN: Tea, anyone?

LISTER: Cheers, man.

KRYTEN: Suggest you don't put your cups on the console, sir. It leaves those ugly little ring marks. Why not use me as a table?

LISTER: I thought you were going to fix yourself.

KRYTEN: Not until I've performed all my duties, sir. I can't go gallivanting off engaging my self-repair unit, not when there's a pile of laundry in the washroom the size of the north face of the Eiger. Besides, the Cat has invited me to the weekly crap game tonight.

CAT: He's gonna be the dice.

RIMMER: Approaching nebula.

LISTER: Let's see what's in there.

53. Model shot. Starbug flies into the gas nebula

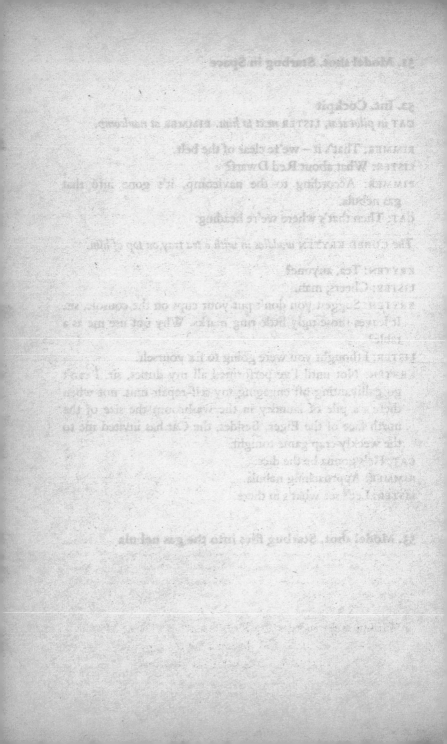

53. Model shot. Starbug in Space

52. Int. Cockpit
CAT in pilot seat, LISTER next to him, RIMMER at rear/console.

RIMMER: That's it – we're clear of the belt.
LISTER: What about Red Dwarf?
RIMMER: According to the navicomp, it's gone into that gas nebula.
CAT: Then that's where we're heading.

The CAMERA travels in with a backswing/top of film.

RIMMER: Tea, anyone?
LISTER: Cheers, man.
RIMMER: Suppose you don't put your cups on the console, sir. It leaves those tacky little ring marks. Why get me me is a table.
LISTER: I thought you were going to fix yourself.
RIMMER: Not until I say I've reported all my duties, sir. I can't go gallivanting off ... toy self-repair units, not when there's a pile of laundry in the washbin/top the size of the tenth tier of the Eiger. Besides, the Cat has turned the to the weekly crap game tonight.
CAT: Hey, count me in the day.
RIMMER: Approaching nebula.
LISTER: Let's see what's in there.

51. Model shot. Starbug flies into the gas nebula

RED DWARF THREE: EPISODE THREE
POLYMORPH

LIST OF EPISODE CREDITS

RED DWARF THREE: EPISODE TWO
MAROONED

Broadcast date: 21 November 1989

Cast:

RIMMER   Chris Barrie
LISTER   Craig Charles
CAT   Danny John Jules
HOLLY   Hattie Hayridge
KRYTEN   Robert Llewellyn

Guest cast:

None

Visual Effects Designer Peter Wragg	*Unit Manager* Janet Smith
Costume Designer Howard Burden	*OB Cameraman* Dave Fox
Make-up Designer Bethan Jones	*Graphic Designer* Mark Allen
Set Designer Mel Bibby	*Camera Supervisor* Dave Hodge
Assistant Set Designer Steve Bradshaw	*Production Manager* Mike Agnew
Lighting Director John Pomphrey	*Production Assistant* Christina Hamilton
Console Operator Dai Thomas	*Assistant Floor Manager* Dona Di Stefano
Sound Supervisor Tony Worthington	*Technical Co-ordinator* Tony Smith
Theme Music Howard Goodall	*Prop Buyer* Sheila McIntyre
Videotape Editor Ed Wooden	*Associate Producer* Gilly Archer

Written and produced by Rob Grant and Doug Naylor
Produced and directed by Ed Bye
Executive Producer Paul Jackson

RED DWARF THREE: EPISODE THREE
POLYMORPH

Broadcast date: 28 November 1989

Cast:

RIMMER   Chris Barrie

LISTER   Craig Charles

CAT   Danny John Jules

HOLLY   Hattie Hayridge

KYRTEN   Robert Llewellyn

Guest cast:

GENNY   Frances Barber

YOUNG RIMMER   Simon Gaffney

MRS RIMMER   Kalli Greenwood

Visual Effects Designer Peter Wragg	*Camera Supervisor* Dave Fox
Costume Designer Howard Burden	*Vision Mixer* Sonia Lovett
Make-up Designer Bethan Jones	*Technical Co-ordinator* Tony Smith
Set Designer Mel Bibby	*Prop Buyer* Stella McIntyre
Assistant Set Designer Steve Bradshaw	*Videotape Editor* Ed Wooden
Lighting Director John Pomphrey	*Assistant Floor Manager* Dona Di Stefano
Console Operator Dai Thomas	*Production Assistant* Christina Hamilton
Sound Supervisor Tony Worthington	*Production Manager* Mike Agnew
Theme Music Howard Goodall	*Associate Producer* Gilly Archer
Unit Manager Janet Smith	

Written and produced by Rob Grant and Doug Naylor
Produced and directed by Ed Bye
Executive Producer Paul Jackson

RED DWARF FOUR: EPISODE THREE
JUSTICE

Broadcast date: 28 February 1991

Cast:

RIMMER	Chris Barrie
LISTER	Craig Charles
CAT	Danny John Jules
HOLLY	Hattie Hayridge
KRYTEN	Robert Llewellyn

Guest cast:

SIMULANT	Nicholas Ball
JUSTICE COMPUTER VO	James Smillie

Visual Effects Peter Wragg
Costume Designer Howard Burden
Make-up Designer Andria Pennell
Set Designer Mel Bibby
Assistant Set Designer Steve Bradshaw
Console Operator Dai Thomas
Lighting Director John Pomphrey
Sound Supervisor Keith Mayes
Theme Music Howard Goodall
Casting Jane Davies
Production Accountant Joanna Birkinshaw
Graphic Designer Paul D'Auria
Production Team Celia Bargh
                   Mairead Curtin

Camera Supervisor Rocket
Vision Mixer Simon Sanders
Vision Supervisor Mike Spencer
Prop Buyer Don Cave
Properties Peter Blackall
Post Production The Edit Works
Videotape Editor Graham Hutchings
Stage Manager Kerry Waddell
Production Assistant Christine Moses
Production Manager Julian Scott
Associate Producer Candida Julian-Jones

Written and produced by Rob Grant and Doug Naylor
Produced and directed by Ed Bye

RED DWARF FIVE: EPISODE FIVE
DIMENSION JUMP

Broadcast date: 14 March 1991

Cast:

RIMMER   Chris Barrie
LISTER   Craig Charles
CAT   Danny John Jules
HOLLY   Hattie Hayridge
KRYTEN   Robert Llewellyn

Guest cast:

MRS RIMMER   Kalli Greenwood
YOUNG RIMMER   Simon Gaffney
COCKPIT COMPUTER   Hetty Baynes

Visual Effects Peter Wragg	*Camera Supervisor* Rocket
Costume Designer Howard Burden	*Post Production* The Edit Works
Make-up Designer Andria Pennell	*Vision Mixer* Simon Sanders
Set Designer Mel Bibby	*Vision Supervisor* Mike Spencer
Assistant Set Designer Steve Bradshaw	*Prop Buyer* Don Cave
Lighting Director John Pomphrey	*Properties* Peter Blackall
Console Operator Dai Thomas	*Videotape Editor* Graham Hutchings
Theme Music Howard Goodall	*Stage Manager* Kerry Waddell
Sound Supervisor Keith Mayes	*Production Assistant* Christine Moses
Casting Jane Davies	*Production Manager* Julian Scott
Production Accountant Joanna Birkinshaw	*Associate Producer* Candida Julian-Jones
Graphic Designer Paul D'Auria	
Production Team Celia Bargh	
Mairead Curtin	

Written and produced by Rob Grant and Doug Naylor
Produced and directed by Ed Bye

RED DWARF FIVE: EPISODE SIX:
BACK TO REALITY

Broadcast date: 26 March 1992

Cast:

RIMMER Chris Barrie
LISTER Craig Charles
CAT Danny John Jules
HOLLY Hattie Hayridge
KRYTEN Robert Llewellyn

Guest cast:

ANDY Timothy Spall
COP Lenny Von Dohlen
NEW KOCHANSKI Anastasia Hille
NURSE Marie McCarthy
NEW LISTER Jake Sharian

Visual Effects Peter Wragg
Costume Designer Howard Burden
Make-up Designer Andria Pennell
Set Designer Mel Bibby
Assistant Set Designer Steve Bradshaw
Lighting Director John Pomphrey
Console Operator Dai Thomas
Sound Supervisor Keith Mayes
Theme Music Howard Goodall
Casting Jane Davies
Production Accountant Joanna Birkinshaw
Unit Manager Irene Gibbons
Video Effects Bruce Steele, Jez Gibson
Production Team Nichol Hoye
Mairead Curtain

Camera Supervisor Rocket
Vision Mixer Simon Sanders
Post Production The Edit Works
Vision Supervisor Mike Spencer
Insert Editor Peter Bates
Gaffer Ron Green
Property Master Mark Hedges
Properties Buyer Stella McIntyre
Technical Manager Jeff Jeffery
Videotape Editor Graham Hutchings
Stage Manager Kerry Waddell
Production Assistant Christine Moses
Associate Producer Julian Scott

Written by Rob Grant and Doug Naylor
Executive Producers Rob Grant and Doug Naylor
Produced by Hilary Beven Jones
Directed by Juliet May, Rob Grant and Doug Naylor

RED DWARF SIX: EPISODE ONE
PSIRENS

Broadcast date: 7 October 1993

Cast:

RIMMER   Chris Barrie
LISTER   Craig Charles
CAT   Danny John Jules
KRYTEN   Robert Llewellyn

Guest cast:

ASTRO   Richard Ridings
TEMPTRESS 1   Zoe Hilson
TEMPTRESS 2   Liz Anson
CAPTAIN TAU   Anita Dobson
KOCHANSKI   C. P. Grogan
PETE TRANTER'S SISTER   Samantha Robson
PROFESSOR MAMET   Jenny Agutter

Visual Effects Peter Wragg
Costume Designer Howard Burden
Make-up Designer Andria Pennell
Set Designer Mel Bibby
Assistant Set Designer Steve Bradshaw
Lighting Director John Pomphrey
Console Operator Dai Thomas
Vision Mixer Simon Sanders
Technical Manager Jeff Jeffery
Prop Master Simon Dalton
Prop Buyer Springer
Casting Jane Davies

Production Accountant Louise Westaway
Floor Assistant Bridget Chick
Stage Manager Rina Konstantinou
Floor Manager Simon Wallace
Post Production The Edit Works
Locations Manager Suzannah Holt
Production Co-ordinator Cressida Sherston
Production Assistant Christine Moses
Production Manager Kerry Waddell
Sound Supervisor Keith Mayes
Theme Music Howard Goodall

Writers and Executive Producers Rob Grant and
Doug Naylor
Director Andy De Emmony
Producer Justin Judd

READ MORE IN PENGUIN

In every corner of the world, on every subject under the sun, Penguin represents quality and variety – the very best in publishing today.

For complete information about books available from Penguin – including Puffins, Penguin Classics and Arkana – and how to order them, write to us at the appropriate address below. Please note that for copyright reasons the selection of books varies from country to country.

In the United Kingdom: Please write to *Dept. JC, Penguin Books Ltd, FREEPOST, West Drayton, Middlesex UB7 OBR*

If you have any difficulty in obtaining a title, please send your order with the correct money, plus ten per cent for postage and packaging, to *PO Box No. 11, West Drayton, Middlesex UB7 OBR*

In the United States: Please write to *Penguin USA Inc., 375 Hudson Street, New York, NY 10014*

In Canada: Please write to *Penguin Books Canada Ltd, 10 Alcorn Avenue, Suite 300, Toronto, Ontario M4V 3B2*

In Australia: Please write to *Penguin Books Australia Ltd, 487 Maroondah Highway, Ringwood, Victoria 3134*

In New Zealand: Please write to *Penguin Books (NZ) Ltd,182–190 Wairau Road, Private Bag, Takapuna, Auckland 9*

In India: Please write to *Penguin Books India Pvt Ltd, 706 Eros Apartments, 56 Nehru Place, New Delhi 110 019*

In the Netherlands: Please write to *Penguin Books Netherlands B.V., Keizersgracht 231 NL–1016 DV Amsterdam*

In Germany: Please write to *Penguin Books Deutschland GmbH, Friedrichstrasse 10–12, W–6000 Frankfurt/Main 1*

In Spain: Please write to *Penguin Books S. A., C. San Bernardo 117–6° E–28015 Madrid*

In Italy: Please write to *Penguin Italia s.r.l., Via Felice Casati 20, I–20124 Milano*

In France: Please write to *Penguin France S. A., 17 rue Lejeune, F–31000 Toulouse*

In Japan: Please write to *Penguin Books Japan, Ishikiribashi Building, 2–5–4, Suido, Bunkyo-ku, Tokyo 112*

In Greece: Please write to *Penguin Hellas Ltd, Dimocritou 3, GR–106 71 Athens*

In South Africa: Please write to *Longman Penguin Southern Africa (Pty) Ltd, Private Bag X08, Bertsham 2013*

READ MORE IN PENGUIN

HUMOUR

Better than Life Grant Naylor

The sequel to the internationally bestselling *Red Dwarf* finds Lister, Rimmer, Cat and Kryten trapped in the ultimate computer game: Better than Life. BTL transports you directly to a perfect world of your imagination, a world where you can enjoy fabulous wealth and unmitigated success. It's the ideal game with only one drawback – it's so good, it will kill you...

The Quest for the Big Woof Lenny Henry and Steve Parkhouse

What is the Big Woof? Perplexed by the question, and with a deadline to meet, Lenny Henry sets off to find the philosopher's stone that turns pain into laughter.

Be a Bloody Train Driver Jacky Fleming

Jacky Fleming takes a wry, original look at women's (and girls') lives in these brilliantly funny cartoons.

Alex V: The Man with the Golden Handshake
Charles Peattie and Russell Taylor

Alex, hero of the *Independent*'s business pages, faces the ultimate indignity: not only has he been made redundant, but people seem to think he has hired his dinner jacket for the charity ball. Meanwhile, Greg, Alex's journalist brother, is roughing it in the desert reporting on the Gulf War ... and claiming expenses for the Riyadh Hilton.

How to Become Ridiculously Well-Read in One Evening E.O. Parrott

Contains some 150 succinct and entertaining encapsulations of the best-known books in the English language, including a few foreign works familiar to us in translation. 'Very funny. Well calculated to put all teachers of English Literature in their places' – John Mortimer

READ MORE IN PENGUIN

A SELECTION OF OMNIBUSES

The Cornish Trilogy   Robertson Davies

'He has created a rich oeuvre of densely plotted, highly symbolic novels that not only function as superbly funny entertainments but also give the reader, in his character's words, a deeper kind of pleasure – delight, awe, religious intimations, "a fine sense of the past, and of the boundless depth and variety of life"' – *The New York Times*

For Good or Evil: Collected Stories   Clive Sinclair

'An ever-changing kaleidoscope of character and scenery and time, some bewilderingly surreal, others starkly cold … powerfully written, extremely clever and very unpleasant' – *The Times*

The Pop Larkin Chronicles   H. E. Bates

'Tastes ambrosially of childhood. Never were skies so cornflower blue or beds so swansbottom … Life not as it is or was, but as it should be' – *Guardian*. 'Pop is as sexy, genial, generous and boozy as ever, Ma is a worthy match for him in these qualities' – *The Times*

The Penguin Book of British Comic Stories
Compiled by Patricia Craig

A rich blend of comic styles ranging from the sunny humour of Wodehouse and the droll comedy of Graham Greene to the grim irony of Fay Weldon and the inventive wit of Muriel Spark.

Lucia Victrix   E. F. Benson

Mapp and Lucia, Lucia's Progress, Trouble for Lucia – now together in one volume, these three chronicles of English country life will delight a new generation of readers with their wry observation and delicious satire.

READ MORE IN PENGUIN

A SELECTION OF OMNIBUSES

The Penguin Book of Modern Women's Short Stories
Edited by Susan Hill

'They move the reader to give a cry of recognition and understanding time and time again' – Susan Hill in the Introduction. 'These stories are excellent. They are moving, wise, and finely conceived ... a selection of stories that anyone should be pleased to own' – *Glasgow Herald*

Great Law-and-Order Stories
Edited and Introduced by John Mortimer

Each of these stories conjures suspense with consummate artistry. Together they demonstrate how the greatest mystery stories enthrall not as mere puzzles but as gripping insights into the human condition.

The Duffy Omnibus   Dan Kavanagh

Nick Duffy – bisexual ex-cop turned private detective – is on the loose, for four rackety adventures in the grimiest streets of old London town... 'Exciting, funny and refreshingly nasty' – *Sunday Times*

The Best of Roald Dahl   Roald Dahl

Twenty tales to curdle your blood and scorch your soul, chosen from his bestsellers *Over to You, Someone Like You, Kiss Kiss* and *Switch Bitch*. *The Best of Roald Dahl* is, quite simply, Roald Dahl at his sinister best!

The Rabbit Novels   John Updike

'One of the finest literary achievements to have come out of the US since the war ... It is in their particularity, in the way they capture the minutiae of the world ... that [the Rabbit] books are most lovable' – John Banville in the *Irish Times*